Good Fishing
in the
Catskills

Good Fishing in the Catskills

A Complete Angler's Guide

Third Edition

Jim Capossela

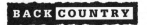

Backcountry Guides
Woodstock, Vermont

An Invitation to the Reader

With time, access points may change and road numbers, signs, and landmarks referred to in this book may be altered. If you find that such changes have occurred, please let the author and publisher know so that corrections may be made in future editions. Other comments and suggestions are also welcome. Address all correspondence to:

Editor
Backcountry Guides
P.O. Box 748
Woodstock, Vermont
05091

Library of Congress Cataloging-in-Publication Data:
Capossela, Jim.
Good fishing in the Catskills : a complete angler's guide / Jim Capossela.—3rd ed.
p. cm.
ISBN 0-88150-508-0
1. Fishing—New York (State)—Catskill Mountains Region. I. Title.
SH529 .C375 2002
799.1'1'0974738—dc21
2001052708

Cover photograph © Richard Franklin
Interior photographs by Jim Capossela unless otherwise noted
Cover and interior design by Faith Hague
Maps drawn by Jim Capossela, © 2002 The Countryman Press
Map Consultant: Larry Boutis

Published by Backcountry Guides
A division of The Countryman Press, P.O. Box 748, Woodstock, VT 05091
Distributed by W. W. Norton & Company, Inc., 500 Fifth Avenue,
New York, NY 10110

Printed in the United States of America
10 9 8 7 6 5 4 3 2 1

The Good Fishing in New York Series

Good Fishing in Lake Ontario and its Tributaries
Good Fishing in the Catskills
Good Fishing in the Adirondacks

By the Same Author

How to Write for the Outdoor Magazines
Good Fishing Close to New York City
Northeast Hunting Guide
Northeast Upland Hunting Guide (with other contributors)
Trophy Trout Streams of the Northeast (editor)
Ice Fishing
Camp and Trail Cooking Techniques
The Palisades
Blue Claw

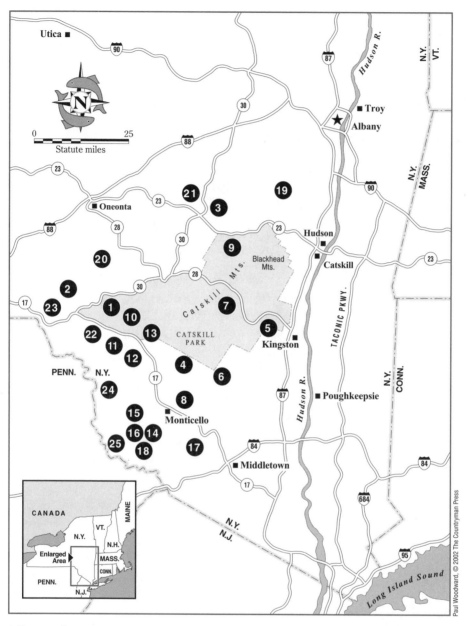

1. Pepacton Reservoir
2. Cannonsville Reservoir
3. Schoharie Reservoir
4. Neversink Reservoir
5. Ashokan Reservoir
6. Rondout Reservoir
7. Esopus Creek
8. Neversink River
9. Schoharie Creek
10. Beaver Kill–Willowemoc
    River System
11. The Lower Beaver Kill
12. The Lower Willowemoc
13. The Upper Willowemoc
14. The Lake District
15. Toronto Reservoir
16. White Lake
17. The Basher Kill
18. Mongaup River System
19. Catskill Creek
20. Northern Delaware County
21. Lower Schoharie County
22. The East Branch Delaware
23. The West Branch Delaware
24. Upper Main Stem
    Delaware
25. Lower Main Stem Delaware

Contents

Preface to the Third Edition

I had my retirement all figured out. Not that it was imminent, but past 50 and one starts thinking about such things.

There'd be no more rain dances on fiendish river rocks, no more waders that started leaking two weeks before they were even manufactured. I'd spent my salad days appropriately enough in the mountains—but didn't all anglers move closer to the sea as their time approached. Hadn't Hemingway? Hadn't McClane?

I would get a small tin boat and put it on the Hudson River, the shores of which, after all, had always been my permanent home. I'd get a dog and put him in the bow of the boat. When my eyes started to go he would bark when a sandbar approached. There would be glorious days on gentle salty winds, with striped bass and bluefish and perch and catfish. No fancy fly tackle here. Just a couple of beat-up old poles, a tackle sack, a thermos of milk, a Geritol capsule. On the Golden Pond of Croton Bay the dog and I would grow old together, and then one day the sun would set over the Palisades for the last time.

And then the phone rang. It seemed that the publisher wanted to bring forth a new edition of a book that I'd already interred in my mind. Wasn't a successful 12 years enough?

The Catskills? I'd seen everything that the mountains had to offer, fished everywhere high and low. They simply held no more surprises for me.

Or so I thought.

Of course there would be updating, but with the enormous task of creating the book out of the way, I was able to turn my attention to some of the finer points. Here, "finer points" meant out-of-the-way places, or—since I'd always been a wanderer—farther out-of-the-way places.

I'd first fished the Catskills exactly 30 years previous. Thus, you might expect that I'd return from this latter-day odyssey with cynicism about hopelessly overcrowded rivers. Actually, nothing could be further from the truth.

What I found was almost all the anglers crowded into just a few rivers, and mile upon mile of smaller water barren but for me and the sweet, languorous river breezes.

It all made sense. Trout fishing had bred a new type of angler. I'd fished 25 years before making it to Montana. Today's well-monied fly-fisher would get to there—if not to Labrador or New Zealand—in his first or second year. He would come back thinking that's the way things are in the real world. Maybe the Delaware would satisfy him. But Woodland Valley Creek? Fir Brook? A hop-across brookie stream? Hah. Not when you were weaned on the Big Horn or the Minipi.

It was startling to find even some of the large and amply famous Catskill rivers clearly underfished. Esopus Creek busy in springtime? Of course. But didn't they know about the cold water below the Portal in summer? A little false-casting on the Neversink from time to time? Granted. But who was fishing below Route 17, let alone in the off-season? As the months of the one-year update advanced, so did my absolute assuredness that at any given moment I could find a solid 2 miles of trout stream for myself.

There seemed to be a parallel imbalance with the big reservoirs. Pepacton had and still has a well-deserved following, but its gorgeous sister to the west—Cannonsville—seemed to be looking for customers. A couple of days I saw its 4,700 acres completely empty. Rondout was drawing a good springtime crowd for its early-season lakers, but its intriguing brother just westward—Neversink Reservoir—seemed to be as lightly fished as ever. And Ashokan—well, that's too big ever to be crowded.

Surprises came at other turns: beaver dams and spanking new brook trout ponds; high-elevation ponds that, while not unfished, still were ingratiating; a walk-in bass lake; a new ice-fishing trout lake; a charming Catskill village that I had never stopped for a beer in. And so it went for the whole year, in the Catskills I'd thought I knew so well.

A reader would normally turn to a new edition's preface to see what has changed, and indeed more has changed than just the imbalanced gravitation to the tailwaters. The expansion of the wild-rainbow fishery in the Delaware–Beaver Kill system is certainly news. So is the unseemly appearance of striped bass (and even gizzard shad) in that same watershed. Species have declined, too. In Ashokan Reservoir, emerald shiners and ciscoes, on the skids a while now, may be history, while the once-famous Ashokan walleyes may now be only remnant. Blame the whole mess on the sawbelly, some say.

The lake trout in Rondout Reservoir have been a thundering success, but the landlocked salmon in Neversink Reservoir are still languishing, or at least not flourishing. This leaves the Catskills without a winning salmon water.

Then there are the waters that everyone wants to fish. Yes, the Delaware and its branches can be crowded now, but even here I can find a little elbow room at carefully selected times, as discussed in the text. Should you find others where you want to fish, there's much good reason to join the queue: Careful fisheries management by the New York State Department of Environmental Conservation (DEC) and (in the West Branch) tons of cold water have fostered a truly superior wild-trout fishery.

Other changes on this important river system? I would cite two: commercialization in the form of full-service fly-fishing resorts, drift-boat guiding, and greater overall tourism in the upper Delaware Valley; and the appearance of one-person pontoon boats, especially on the main stem.

I would be remiss if I didn't mention the great January flood of 1996. Heavy rains and warm temperatures melted a 20-inch snowpack almost overnight, and the result was surely one of the worst floods of the 20th century. Streams with embedded clay strata, especially the West Kill, saw severe erosion, and some smaller streams like Russell Brook were carved as much as 5 feet deeper in places. It was awesome to get to the mountains a few days after this flood and witness what it had done. Many conservation groups were further dismayed by the bulldozing that was subsequently done on the headwater streams to attempt to reopen roads and bridges and otherwise mitigate the effects of the big washout. While many of the small headwaters will never look the same—both because of the flood and because of the repair work—it seems as if most of the affected midsized streams are now healing nicely.

Finally, the Catskills themselves are slowly changing. I think first of the transmogrification of Main Street from hardware stores and coffee shops into antiques dens and real estate offices. Yes, New York City money has found the Catskills, but even this draws only a sardonic smile from me: By simply avoiding the more popular rivers, I automatically avoid the villages and hamlets where these undesired changes are occurring.

I'll come right out and say it: The lower East Branch of the Delaware has long been my home water. It's a river that I still truly love, but in a modern age, mating for life is getting harder to do. Gone were the days when I could fish alone my favorite mile of this glorious trout stream, but would I ever find a new soul mate?

And then one day during this past year I came across it: the stream that was sent to earth for my personal benediction. It's not too big but not too small, and its trout are all wild. The setting is exquisite. Few know of it.

In any case, a guidebook must be totally candid to be true to its mission, and thus you will find a full description of that stream on page 225.

Acknowledgments

I wish to extend a special thanks to the New York State Department of Environmental Conservation for its tremendous support in the creation of this book, and in its updating. Following are the individuals with the DEC who helped with this or earlier editions: Wayne Elliot, Ron Pierce, Mike Flaherty, Bob Angyal, Andy Kahnle, Ed Van Put, Tim Backus, Kathy Hatala, Russ Fieldhouse, Don Slingerland, Doug Carlson, Norm McBride, Walt Keller, Kay Sanford, Les Wedge, Bill Kelly, Jake Arthur, and Doug Sheppard.

Once again the Upper Delaware River Unit of the National Park Service made available its expert staff to answer questions and proofread the chapter on the main stem of the Delaware. I can personally thank Sandra Schultz, Mike Reuber, and John Hutsky; other NPS employees also helped.

Larry Boutis not only posed for the cover shot of earlier editions but also provided more tangible service with the interior of the book. He created the map standards and many of the rough maps for both this book and other volumes in the Good Fishing in New York series.

Other friends and associates who helped are the Pennsylvania Fish and Boat Commission, Dorri Rosen of the New York Botanical Garden library, Dan Vorisek of the Frost Valley YMCA, Peggy Cardillo, Alice Vera, Tom Schlichter, Tina Schlichter, Charlie Somolofski, Harry Wirtz, Tom Lake, Ron Kolodziej, Bob McNitt, and Ed Noonan.

Since the research for the first edition of this book occurred more than a dozen years ago, I may have forgotten a name or two, and there were innumerable sport shop owners, anglers, and other experts whose names I never got but who provided some of the most essential information.

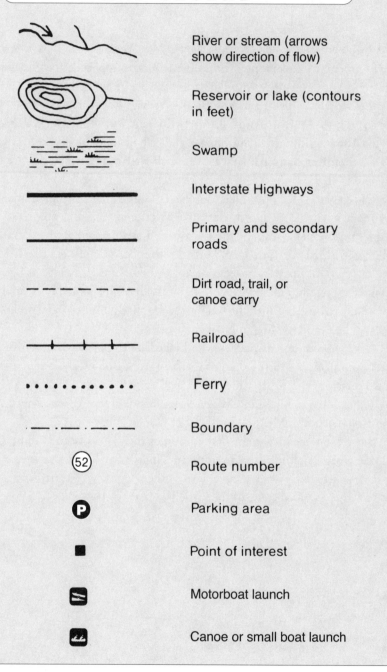

MAP LEGEND

River or stream (arrows show direction of flow)

Reservoir or lake (contours in feet)

Swamp

Interstate Highways

Primary and secondary roads

Dirt road, trail, or canoe carry

Railroad

Ferry

Boundary

Route number

Parking area

Point of interest

Motorboat launch

Canoe or small boat launch

Warning!

The New York State Department of Health warns that many fish in New York waters have elevated levels of certain potentially harmful contaminants. Consult the New York State Department of Environmental Conservation for further details. Many of the current advisories will be seen on the inside front cover of the DEC annual publication, *New York State Fishing Regulations Guide.*

CHAPTER 1

Monsters of the Mountain Reservoirs

To truly know the Catskills is to shiver hopelessly all night long on Pepacton Reservoir, praying for dawn—only to learn that the coldest hour of all is when first light pushes across a shale-blue desolation. The madness of the giant brown pushes a person to his physical limits, but only when he goes a little beyond those limits may he feel the awesome throb of a hook-jawed leviathan on the end of his line. A 20-pound brown is at once a creature of exquisite beauty and an ugly, two-headed dragon to be slain. And monsters of such proportions indeed swim in the mountain reservoirs.

Depicted on figure 1.1, they are, from largest to smallest, Ashokan, Pepacton, Cannonsville, Rondout, Neversink, and Schoharie. They are cold, deep, generally clear and clean, stark and wild looking, undeveloped along

Note: Immediately after the September 11, 2001 terrorist attacks, the New York City Department of Environmental Protection (DEP) suspended all fishing and boating on all of its Catskill and downstate reservoirs, and on many if not all streams that flow through city property. Other water supply reservoirs in the region may also have experienced closures. Given the uncertainties that exist at the time of this writing in late 2001, no projection can be made as to when these waters will be reopened, or what new restrictions might apply when they are reopened. For current information on this situation, contact one of the DEP offices listed on page 20.

their banks, and they are all part of the New York City watershed system. They contain four kinds of trout, one kind of salmon, two kinds of black bass, and both pickerel and walleyes. There are also "rough fish" and panfish, though few seek these when game fish of such sizes are available.

These waters and their fishing are best described separately, but a few collective comments can be made. First is the subject of permits. These reservoirs are open to all, New York State residents as well as nonresidents, but all anglers 16 years of age or older must obtain a free watershed permit. The permit remains good for five years, except for those issued prior to April 9, 1993, and marked VALID UNTIL REVOKED, which are lifetime. Several watershed offices issue permits; they are summarized on page 20. These offices are generally open Monday through Friday during business hours, but it would be best to call the office you plan to visit to verify this. You must appear in person, and you must bring the following:

(1) Proof of identification indicating that you are 16 years of age or older;
(2) A current resident or nonresident New York State fishing license.

Children under 16 years of age may fish the watershed without a permit, but only when they are accompanied by an adult who does have one.

While you may fish any of the reservoirs from shore, you can also choose to fish from a boat. No motors of any kind are allowed—only rowboats. Canoes are not permitted. Day-to-day cartopping is forbidden. Your boat must remain chained to a tree on shore, and it must be "inspected" each year. I doubt they actually do this, but the formality requires that you send in your boating permit each year so that officials can stamp it. Boating permits are also free, and are good for five years, renewable thereafter. For more information, inquire at any of the watershed offices listed. Staff members there will give you a brochure that summarizes the rules and regulations pertaining to boating and to the watershed in general.

In recent times state officials have found mercury in the water of most or all of the reservoirs. I have been told that this is atmospheric in origin. If this is the case, then mercury must logically be found in most other fresh waters in the region. Smallmouth bass are said to have the highest levels of mercury. The city has begun distributing a brochure that talks about the possible risks of eating fish from the waters it administers.

A warning regarding the eating of freshwater fish from New York State

Fig. 1.1 New York City Reservoir Statistics

GAME FISH OPPORTUNITIES

SEASON AND DAILY TAKE LIMITS
(Also see official "Fishing Regulations Guide" for possible changes and additional rules and regulations)

	DATE COMPLETED	SIZE (ACRES)	MAX. DEPTH (FEET)	AVE. DEPTH (FEET)	Season	Daily Take Limits	PRINCIPAL FORAGE FISH PRESENT	BROWN TROUT	LAKE TROUT	RAINBOW TROUT	LARGEMOUTH BASS	SMALLMOUTH BASS	CHAIN PICKEREL	LANDLOCKE SALMON	WALLEYE
ASHOKAN	1913	8321	171	49	Trout: 4/1–11/30 Walleye: First Saturday in May to March 15	3 fish; 12" minimum 3 fish; 18" minimum	• ALEWIFE	E		G		E			F
SCHOHARIE	1926	1146	130	57	Trout: All year	3 fish; 12" minimum	• YELLOW PERCH • ALEWIFE	F	E		F	G			E
RONDOUT	1944	2100	180	77	Trout: 4/1–11/30 Lake trout: 4/1–11/30	3 fish; 12" minimum 3 fish; 18" minimum	• ALEWIFE	G				G			
NEVERSINK	1953	1500	164	80	Trout: 4/1–10/15 Landlocked salmon: 4/1–10/15 Smelt fishing prohibited	3 fish; 12" minimum 3 fish; 15" minimum	• ALEWIFE • SMELT	G				G	F	F	
PEPACTON	1955	5700	170	79	Trout: 4/1–9/30	2 fish to include only one over 21"	• ALEWIFE	E				G		F	
CANNONSVILLE	1963	4750	130	61	Trout: 4/1–10/15	3 fish; 12" minimum	• ALEWIFE	E			F	G	G		

E=EXCELLENT G=GOOD F=FAIR

Fishing permits only are available year-round Monday through Friday, 9–5, at offices 1 and 2 below. Both fishing and boating permits are available March 15 through October 15 at offices 3 through 7, Tuesday through Saturday, 8–4:30.

1. NYC DEP One Stop Center
   59–17 Junction Boulevard, first floor
   Corona, NY 11368
   (718) 595-4820

2. NYC DEP Bureau of Customer Conservation Services
   1250 Broadway, eighth floor
   New York, NY 10001
   (212) 643-2215

3. East of Hudson Permit Office (east of Hudson reservoir boat permits only)
   54 Croton Falls Road
   Mahopac, NY 10541
   (914) 232-1309

4. Grahamsville Permit Office (Rondout and Neversink Reservoirs boat permits only)
   NYS Route 42
   Grahamsville, NY 12740
   (845) 985-2524

5. Ashokan Permit Office (Ashokan Reservoir boat permits only)
   NYS Route 28A
   Shokan, NY 12481
   (845) 657-2663

6. Schoharie Permit Office
   Between Prattsville and Grand Gorge
   (607) 588-6631

7. Downsville Permit Office (Pepacton and Cannonsville Reservoir boat permits only)
   NYS Route 30
   Downsville, NY 13755
   (607) 363-7009 or 363-7010

waters is posted in the beginning of this book, but for more complete information you should contact the New York State Departments of Health or Environmental Conservation.

If you're new to the reservoirs, you might wonder: Do I really need a boat? Generally speaking, there is some very good shore activity for trout in early spring, from ice-out until early or mid-May. This appears to be the time, during open season, when trout are most apt to be prowling the shoreline. After early or mid-May, the water warms quickly and thermal stratification occurs in most of the reservoirs; then, you need a boat if you expect to score with any consistency. A few specific techniques will be discussed later in this chapter.

If you seek bass on these waters, you'll be pleased to find very, very few other anglers in pursuit of them. Why? For one thing, bass boats with their motors are forbidden. For another, the excellent trout fishing seems to overshadow the black bass. But just because you can't bring your bass boat doesn't mean you can't row for largemouths and smallmouths. When the water level is down, you can certainly walk the shoreline and do quite well casting bait or lures. But if the water is up, it will be impossible to walk the shoreline in most parts of the reservoirs. You'll only be able to poke in for a cast here and there. All in all, you can find some excellent smallmouth fishing and some limited largemouth fishing, but a boat is highly recommended.

The other important game fish is the walleye, which is found in good numbers in Schoharie. There is some concerted shoreline activity for this bottom-hugging fish in spring and fall, but the best stringers of glasseyes fall to the boat angler who has so much more command of the water. The reservoir regulations on game fish are largely the same as the statewide regulations, but there are some exceptions; see figure 1.1.

Ice fishing is not expressly permitted on any of the Catskill watershed reservoirs. How this affront to cold-water anglers is allowed to be, I do not know. Ice fishing is allowed on almost all of the Westchester and Putnam reservoirs, and I see no reason why it should not also be permissible in the Catskills.

What about spawning runs of fish from these reservoirs up into tributary streams? In Pepacton, Cannonsville, Ashokan, and Rondout you would be wise to look to tributary mouths and the lower ends of the tributaries in autumn before the season closes (this varies by reservoir). Prespawning browns will gravitate toward the rivers as soon as late August, even though most spawning takes place between October 15 and November 25. From

Ashokan, both rainbow trout and brown trout ascend Esopus Creek during fall and/or spring. These exciting opportunities are discussed in chapter 2. Beyond that, wandering trout from the reservoirs might be randomly found in a given tributary at almost any time.

Pepacton

This is the flagship of the Catskill sextet, and it has made a whole lot of headlines since soon after its completion in the mid-1960s. It's easily the best brown trout reservoir in the city chain, and in fact one of the best in the entire Northeast. Browns taken here average about 17 inches, while the biggest rod-and-reel catches I have heard of were 20 to 22 pounds. Conservation department biologists have netted browns up to 18 pounds. Trout over 15 pounds are very uncommon, though, and in the most recent season the largest fish taken of which I am aware was 14 pounds—still an eye-popping trout. This is typically about the biggest reported taken in a given year, but there are probably a lot of big fish we never hear about. Many of the best fishermen keep their mouths shut.

Pepacton is about 20 miles long and averages 0.5 mile wide. When at full pool, the reservoir encompasses 5,700 acres and is 1,280 feet above sea level. Draining a lightly settled and relatively unspoiled region, Pepacton is extremely clear and well oxygenated. The oxygen is so good, in fact, that trout have been found at all levels all the way down to the bottom—160 feet. The water is very clean and alga blooms are infrequent and sparse. Only near the inlet of the East Branch Delaware do they regularly occur, usually in July and August.

Pepacton is stocked annually with about 10,000 browns, and these account for some 30 percent of all fish taken by anglers. Hatchery fish are usually easier to catch, however, so this statistic may not speak accurately to the percentage of wild fish in Pepacton. In at least one net survey, some 86 percent of the trout captured were of wild origin. Virtually every tributary supports some spawning. and all or almost all of the really big browns taken from Pepacton are wild fish.

Brown trout eggs laid and fertilized in a tributary stream hatch the following spring. The juvenile trout stay in their natal stream for two years before migrating down to the reservoir at an average size of 7 to 9 inches. Once in the lake, the browns grow extremely fast on a sawbelly diet, putting on perhaps 12 inches and 3 pounds of weight in a year's time. This is an

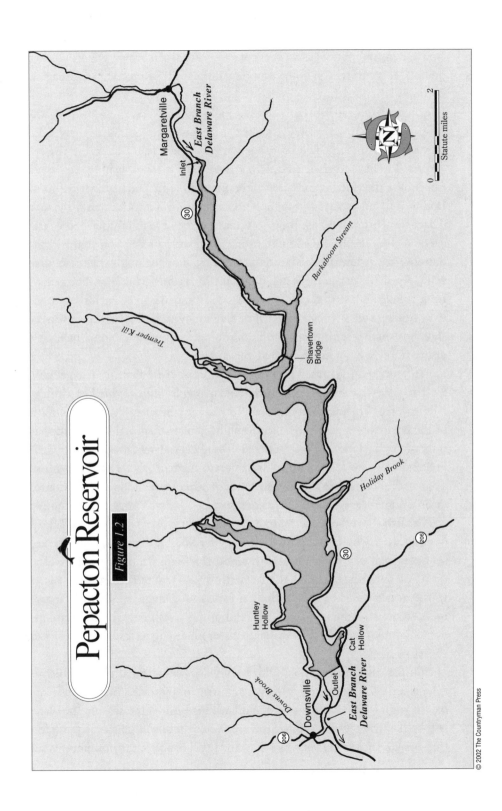

Pepacton Reservoir

Figure 1.2

Margaretville

East Branch Delaware River

Inlet

30

Barkaboom Stream

Trenper Kill

Shavertown Bridge

Holiday Brook

206

30

Huntley Hollow

Downs Brook

Cat Hollow

Downsville

Outlet

East Branch Delaware River

206

N

0 2

Statute miles

© 2002 The Countryman Press

amazing growth rate! At five years of age, a Pepacton brown will be about 8 pounds. If it survives to nine years (few do), it will be pushing that magical 20-pound mark.

Shore fishing at Pepacton is very popular and reasonably productive early in spring. More than once I've gotten to Pepacton at 11 P.M. in early April only to find skim ice slowly creeping out from shore. In the dark, I have been surprised to have my bait land with a *thud!* This is tough fishing, but if you can endure the cold your chances of hooking up with a nice brown are good. If you can't gut it out the whole night, come at 3 A.M. and fish till 7 A.M. That's very often the best time. You may not be able to buy sawbellies this early in the season, but regular shiners will work. Keep your bait on the bottom with as few split shot as possible. This shore fishing works best up to about April 30. While night and especially predawn are the best times, many trout are also taken in the daytime. Cloudy, rainy days can be tops, but anglers beach some fish even on bright and sunny days. Also in early season, shoreline casting with flashy, wobbling spoons can produce some fish. Cast just to the side of a visible wake on the surface.

In years past, Huntley Hollow looked like a little floating village, with Coleman lanterns from several dozen boats flooding the night. The strategy here involves anchoring and suspending one or two lanterns over the side of the boat; this is accomplished through the use of special hooks propped into empty oarlocks. The lanterns almost always attract schooling sawbellies, and the browns in turn are drawn up to the baitfish. Most fish with an open bail, the line held from free-falling with a Strike Guard—a patented device. Sometimes a barrel sinker as heavy as $1/4$ or $1/2$ ounce is used to keep the baitfish down between 10 to 35 feet (presumably just below the school of attracted sawbellies). If you minimize the weight, however, you will present your bait in a more natural way, and you'll enjoy more hook-ups. Put on just a split shot and let the sawbelly swim where it pleases. This, of course, will cause more tangled lines if two or more anglers, each fishing two rods, are present in the boat. This kind of night fishing, which I'm told is not as popular as it once was, seems to produce bigger browns than does shoreline fishing.

Drift fishing from a boat with a single sawbelly can also draw fine results. I was out one day in April when a woman who was, like me, drifting bait in Cat Hollow caught a 14-pounder. This early in the season, the water will be relatively uniform in temperature, but there will be subtle temperature breaks, and it will pay to try to find these with a thermometer. Fre-

The reservoirs have to be drawn down only about 10 feet or so before good smallmouth cover is revealed. Mark these spots on your map, then come back with the bait or lure of your choice. Shown here: a September morning on Pepacton.

quently, trout will hover around the top of a temperature break. Later a thermocline will set up, and then you can start seeking that 58- to 60-degree temperature that the brown favors. Using the wind to your advantage, you can cover a lot of water; just remember that you'll have to row back from wherever you're blown to.

Since motors are prohibited, relatively few people use downriggers, but other Great Lakes strategies have been imported. For example, many bait-fishermen now use long noodle rods of $10^{1}/_{2}$ to 11 feet set up with a spinning reel and 6-pound-test line. Those who like to consistently lose all their big fish use cheap spinning reels. Those who prefer to catch the 8-pound-and-better trout that they hook use top-quality spinning reels with ultrasmooth drags. Legendary fisherman Jack Dykstra, who has caught some of the biggest browns ever taken in the watershed, uses, or at one time did use, an expensive Fin-Nor fly reel because of its extremely smooth drag.

Trolling seems to be the most consistently productive method after June 1. It's easy to see the Lake Ontario influence on this method. Sophisticated graphite rods and line-counting reels have replaced a lot of the clunky conventional tackle that held down the fort in Pepacton's formative days. Great

Lakes lures are here, too. In one recent season, a straight green Thunderstick was hot for trolling; in another season it might be a different lure. Most successful trollers use lead-core line, and many rely on depth sounders and electronic thermometers. Many of the expert trollers I know shun cowbells and other complex rigs and use a single spoon, sometimes with just a single hook. One popular flutter spoon in these parts is the Leatherstocking in copper/nickel or all nickel.

Smallmouth bass fishing in Pepacton is excellent and very much underutilized. The fish average about $1\frac{1}{2}$ to 3 pounds, but battling bronzebacks of 6 pounds are taken by the better fishermen.

The formula for smallmouths is quite simple: Look for shoreline rocks where hide the crawfish that smallmouths love. Best tactic is to use a boat and cast toward shore where there are rocky escarpments or just large boulders. Rocky areas may also be found near the mouths of certain tributaries, such as where the Tremper Kill enters. I once caught a 24-inch pickerel at this spot, rather a surprise. Near the dam, one shoreline where there is a lot of prime, rocky habitat is that section on the south shore just east of Cat Hollow. Live crawfish are absolutely tops. Deep-running crankbaits that simulate crawfish are also effective. In early morning, when the mist is heavy along the lake, try trolling parallel to shore with a floater-diver such as a Rebel or Rapala. An excellent time to try for Pepacton bronzebacks is September, when the water cools surprisingly fast and the fish become very cooperative. These misty, late-summer and early-autumn mornings show off this lake at its best.

Largemouths are found in some of the coves but would be considered uncommon. Those infrequently caught pickerel find just as little suitable habitat here.

Few people fish Pepacton specifically for panfish, although a few different species are present. Brown bullheads are plentiful and will sometimes fool you by grabbing your sawbelly. Yellow perch and rock bass are present in small sizes. The thieving rock bass will pick off many of your live crawfish when you're casting for smallmouths. I've heard one or two reports of crappies also being present.

Year in and year out, the period around Memorial Day is a hot time for browns on this reservoir. Shore fishing has mainly ended by this time, but night fishing, drifting, trolling, and even anchoring with bait will take a lot of fish. Following this, the first two weeks of June can also be very fruitful. Then warmer water puts the fish deeper and skillful trolling becomes a good

Pepacton Reservoir is one of the best brown trout lakes in the east.
The six-pounder in this net is only a ho-hum specimen here.

method. Although early morning can always be good, one expert here told me that evening, beginning right around 7 P.M., is often choice.

A well-stocked bait and tackle shop is located right near the Pepacton dam at the eastern fringe of Downsville. Another place for tackle and advice is the Tremper Kill store a few miles up toward Andes from Shavertown Bridge.

Cannonsville

This is a stunningly beautiful reservoir, tucked into a stark, unspoiled Delaware County valley. Cannonsville is a few years younger than Pepacton, having been filled only since 1968. This reservoir is about 15 miles long and 0.5 mile wide on average. Its maximum depth is about 140 feet, while the average depth is 61 feet. Cannonsville lies 1,150 feet above sea level.

It is clearly not as good a brown trout lake as cleaner Pepacton, but it's not a slouch, either, since fish of over 20 pounds have been reported. In the season just past, the trout fishing here was reported as very good.

Cannonsville is only a little smaller than Pepacton, but it possesses a much smaller year-round trout zone since oxygen levels aren't as good. The real problem is that heavy nutrient loads are present in runoff to Cannonsville (principally from the West Branch Delaware River, upon which it was formed), and these nutrients—especially phosphorous—stimulate dense alga blooms during summer. When this algae decays, it removes dissolved oxygen from much of the water column during July, August, and September. The result is that only the deeper water in the lower end of the reservoir has sufficient oxygen to sustain trout during summer months. From October to June, dissolved oxygen levels are adequate in most of the lake, so those afloat during these times can spread out and try the very same tactics described under "Pepacton."

Growth rates for browns are similar to those found in Pepacton, but the browns taken in Cannonsville are almost all wild fish spawned in the tributaries. Smallmouths are also abundant here, and since the overall angling pressure is light it's logical to assume that the bass are pursued even less here than in Pepacton. Perch, bullheads, and rock bass are present in Cannonsville, and (unlike Pepacton) there are also substantial numbers of carp present in the shallower coves. Largemouth bass and pickerel are present, too, but neither species makes headlines here.

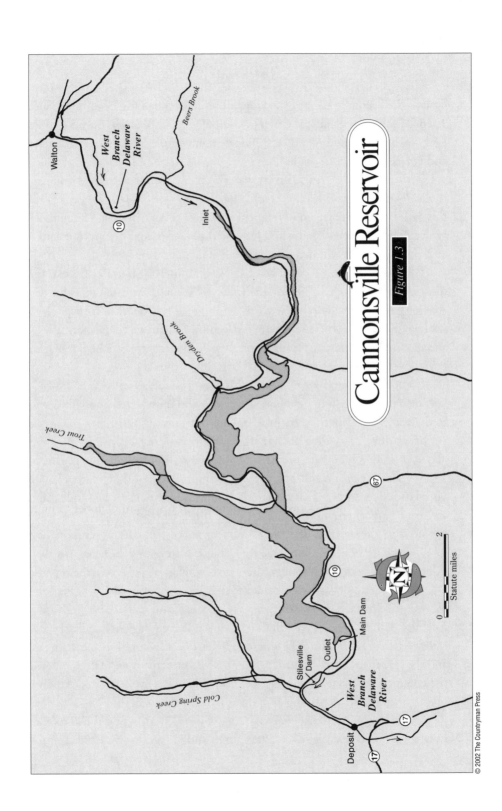

Cannonsville Reservoir

Figure 1.3

Schoharie

This is the second oldest of the Catskill reservoirs, having been filled since 1926. Much smaller than the two just discussed, Schoharie is only 5.8 miles long, with a maximum depth of 130 feet. It encompasses 1,145 surface acres and is 1,130 feet above sea level.

This reservoir serves to divert water from the Schoharie River drainage to Ashokan Reservoir via the Shandaken Tunnel (see chapter 2). Because of this, Schoharie is subjected to frequent water-level fluctuations. Although it's typically full between March and June, withdrawals usually begin thereafter, and a maximum drawdown of 40 to 60 feet can occur by late fall.

Schoharie supports a very good self-sustaining warm-water fishery, the most important game fish being the walleye. At one time catch rates for this species compared favorably with those in some of New York State's best walleye lakes. The average glasseye taken by Schoharie fishermen is only about 15 to 17 inches, but trophies of 10 to 13 pounds are beached or boated nearly every season. They are all wild fish.

Sometime around 1990, or possibly a bit sooner, alewives (aka sawbellies) made their way into Schoharie Reservoir and immediately posed a threat to the walleye population. As in Ashokan, the alewives were seen to eat the young walleye fry, which at that stage of growth are planktonic. By 1995 alewives were already abundant, and walleye numbers were down. But in 1996—possibly as a result of the great January flood of that year—alewife populations plummeted, and there is evidence that in the years following, walleye numbers rebounded. In fact, some DEC electrofishing in 1997 confirmed this, and verified that there had been successful natural reproduction in 1996 and 1997. As of late 2000 the walleye fishing in Schoharie was considered "very good," even though there is somewhat of a cloud in the picture.

When the walleyes are not paradoxically being eaten by baitfish, the baitfish they like to eat is the yellow perch. (Can you blame them? Few freshwater fish taste better.) Yellows are still the primary walleye forage in Schoharie, and the two fish are thought to be interdependent: The perch feed the walleyes, and the walleyes in turn control perch numbers effectively enough to prevent the common problem of stunting. Yellows taken here average 8 to 10 inches in length, and provide fishing as good as that for the walleye.

In his book *Complete Guide to Walleye Fishing*, Art Moraski claims that walleyes do indeed suspend at certain times and in certain situations. But the

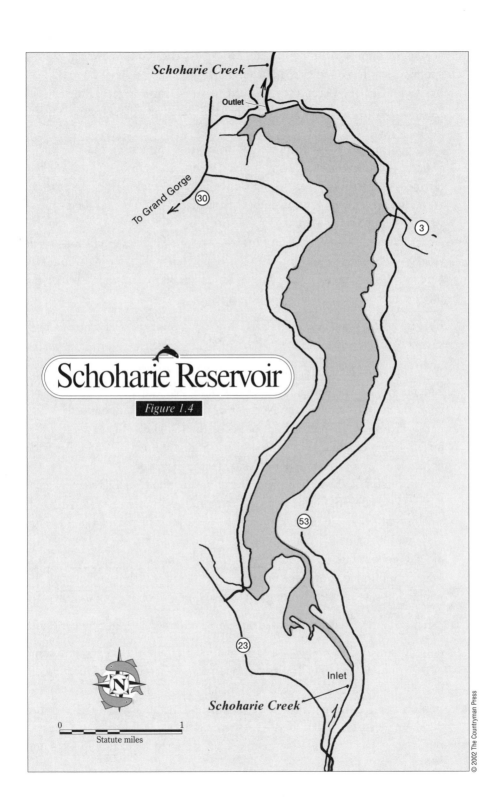

Schoharie Creek

Outlet

To Grand Gorge ③⓪

③

Schoharie Reservoir

Figure 1.4

⑤③

②③

Inlet

Schoharie Creek

N

0   1
Statute miles

general wisdom is that the fish is almost exclusively a bottom dweller. During summer Schoharie walleyes are taken most often at depths of 10 to 30 feet. Walleyes, like the perch they stalk, very often travel together in schools. Smart fishermen get their line back into the water very quickly after a fish is boated.

Smallmouth bass are present but are less numerous than in either Pepacton or Cannonsville. Crawfish are, again, a superb bait, but if you're a lure person you should come equipped with diving crankbaits or jigs that can represent the sulking, bottom-hugging crawdads. Autumn is a good time of year for Schoharie smallmouths.

A relatively small number of brown trout—2,100 in a recent season—is stocked in Schoharie and provides fair opportunity. That rating would also apply to the largemouth bass. Brown bullheads, carp, and rock bass are the other common finny creatures in this reservoir.

Neversink

At 1,500 acres Neversink is the second smallest Catskill reservoir, being larger only than Schoharie. It has long been known as one of the purest reservoirs, its main tributary—the Neversink River, which it impounded—emanating from the unspoiled high peaks of the Catskills. Shaped like a big, upside-down comma, Neversink is about 5 miles long and 1.25 miles wide at its widest point. It sits at about 1,500 feet in elevation.

Neversink is the only body of water within the Catskills managed for landlocked salmon. Game fish occurring naturally here are brown trout, smallmouth bass, and pickerel. For many years after its completion in 1955, Neversink remained virtually unfished. At that time, there was a population of wild brown trout, no doubt progeny of river fish that one day found themselves impounded. But since browns weren't stocked (they still aren't), the population was apparently not great and so anglers seeking big trout looked to Ashokan Reservoir, or to Pepacton.

The genesis of the salmon stocking program was in 1971. In that year rainbow smelt, *Osmerus mordax*, were planted, in the form of eggs, into some of the tributary streams. Biologists hoped the smelt would provide a forage base for the soon-to-be-stocked salmon. This phase of the program went extremely well, and smelt runs were established in the Neversink River and other smaller tribs. Then in 1973 Atlantic salmon, *Salmo salar* or true sea-run salmon, were put into Neversink. They were stocked again in 1974 and

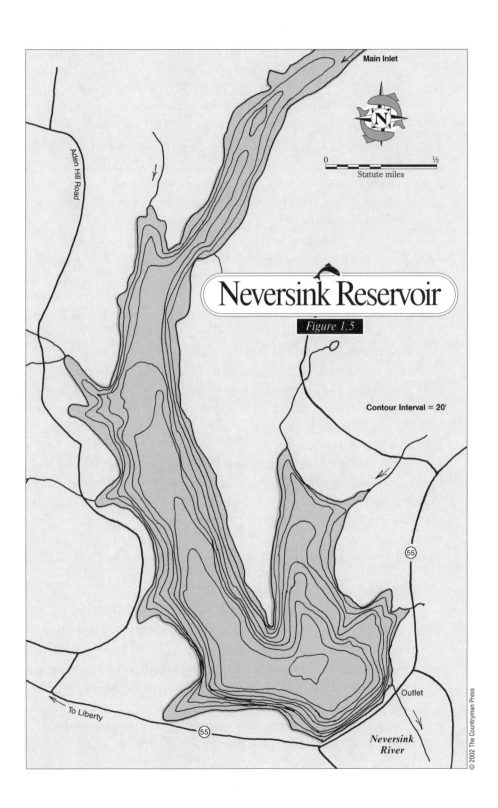

Main Inlet

0 ——————————— ½
Statute miles

Aden Hill Road

Neversink Reservoir

Figure 1.5

Contour Interval = 20'

55

To Liberty

55

Outlet

Neversink River

'75 but didn't take hold. In the late 1970s the DEC tried landlocked salmon *(Salmo salar sebago),* and stocking of this sport fish has continued to this day. It's a program that has drawn mixed results. Since 1983, 3,000 yearling salmon have been planted each spring in the reservoir; survival has been variable, with the fish doing better in some years than in others, but with some natural reproduction apparently occurring. Beginning in the late 1990s fingerling salmon have been occasionally stocked directly into the Neversink River above the reservoir, in the hope that these will "smolt" or imprint to the chemistry of the stream before migrating downstream, so that they will be impelled to return when they're old enough to spawn.

Through the years many landlocks have been taken by anglers from Neversink's crystalline waters, but neither the numbers nor the sizes have been overly impressive. Still, angler use of the reservoir is so light that accurately assessing the quality of the fishing is difficult. Neversink is far from any population center and, unlike Pepacton, is not in the heart of the Catskills; thus, it isn't utilized by many weekend residents (many weekenders keep a boat on Pepacton). Brown trout may currently be about as numerous as salmon.

Statewide regulations on landlocks prevail here: 15 inches minimum and three fish per day. The season is the same as for trout, that is, April 1 through October 15. To protect the salmon's food stock, smelt fishing is prohibited. Nonetheless, alewives probably constitute the primary source of food for salmonids in this reservoir.

The first real crack at the Neversink salmon occurs in April. Smelt leave their (presumably deep) winter haunts and move toward the feeder streams that they will soon ascend to spawn. The mostly local people who try at this time fish live bait such as shiners, sawbellies, or nightcrawlers. Baitfish-imitating spoons, spinners, and swimming plugs cast near the tributaries can also nail a salmon or even a brown. Browns follow the smelt inshore in spring, too.

After the short but concentrated smelt run ends, browns and salmon tend to spread out along the shoreline and can be taken with bait or lures. Some anglers suspend a baitfish a few feet below the surface with the aid of a bobber.

As spring advances, both the trout and the salmon move deeper, and trolling from a boat becomes the predominant method. Nonetheless, there is reputed to be some summer activity with salmon at night near tributary mouths.

As mentioned, smallmouth bass are present in Neversink, and also—according to resident experts—some huge chain pickerel. The smallmouth are often found near rocks, as discussed under "Pepacton." The pickerel will usually be found on the shallow, weedy flats, which pretty much means the upper end of the reservoir. Still, both bass and pickerel have been taken out in the main part of the lake during netting surveys. Doubtless, the sawbellies have drawn them there. Every so often you'll hear about a brookie in the 18- to 21-inch class having been taken from this still largely ignored impoundment.

Certain watershed officials in this part of the Catskills are of the thinking that the relatively few people who fish Neversink are quite content that the reservoir is neither overpublicized nor overfished. Do they have a good thing going? Besides the allure of wild fish, there is also the fact that the back part of Neversink is very wild, and far from any road. Here the Neversink River as well as a few other tributaries come on board. Though I haven't been afloat on this reservoir, I am always attracted to out-of-the-way places, and the back or northern half of Neversink provides that temptation.

Because of its north–south orientation, Neversink is highly subject to windy conditions, blowing anglers off the main part of the lake many days. This can loom especially large if you're traveling a fair distance to fish here.

Ashokan

Ashokan is an enormous body of water, covering just over 8,300 surface acres. It is as much as 2.25 miles wide and 171 feet deep at the maximum. It's not only the largest of the Catskill reservoirs, by a considerable margin, but also the oldest. It lies 600 feet above sea level.

It's hard to believe that even a thirst as great as New York City's could put a dent in this immense inland sea. Yet in one recent year, the east basin of Ashokan was drawn down more than 50 feet. Pictures of this drawdown may have vividly come into your living room, since it was reported by several major TV stations covering the drought that year.

Ashokan is divided roughly in half by a low, rounded stone dam that I'll refer to hereafter as the weir. The two basins are sometimes called upper and lower, but I'll use the terms *east basin* and *west basin,* which should avoid any confusion.

Fish certainly can slip over the dam from the west basin into the east basin, and during high water, larger fish, especially trout, can make a leap and go in the other direction. In addition, there is a subsurface conduit connecting the two basins by which fish can sometimes make passage. Thus, any fish that occurs in one basin can and eventually will occur in the other.

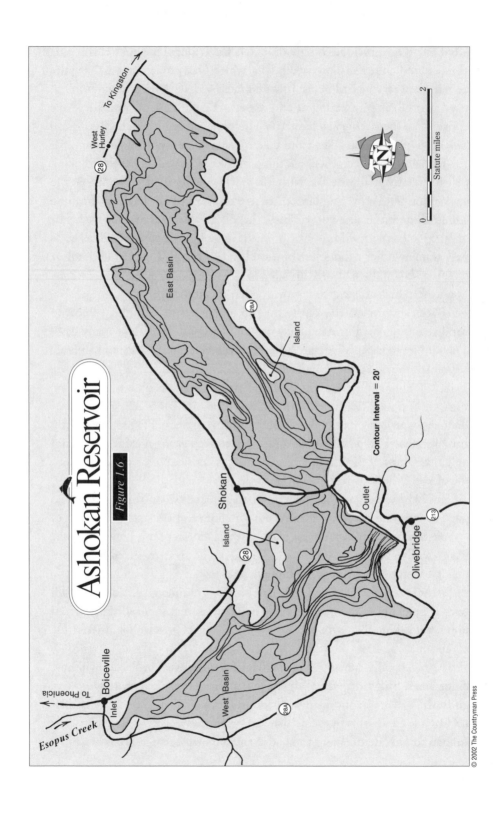

Ashokan Reservoir

Figure 1.6

East Basin

West Basin

Island

Island

Esopus Creek

To Phoenicia

Boiceville

Inlet

Shokan

West Hurley

To Kingston

Oliliebridge

Outlet

Contour Interval = 20'

Statute miles

N

28

28A

28A

213

By a wide margin, the game fish most hotly pursued here is the brown trout. These silver-and-gold-flanked beauties occur in both basins, but local bait shop owners tell me that the east basin is by far the better one. One popular mooring spot is in the northwest corner of the east basin. In recent years the city has begun to label popular mooring areas on the reservoirs, and this one is designated E-2. Anglers mooring boats in either basin here use the parking spaces just north of the bridge dividing the basins.

Ashokan is such a large lake that there is no hope of simply rowing to the current "hot spot" in all instances. For example, if you keep a boat at the extreme eastern end of the east basin, you'll be growing a beard by the time you row down to the dam dividing the basins. For this reason, talk to local experts—including tackle shop owners—and choose your mooring spot well. The western portion of the east basin is indeed a perennial hot spot for browns, although certainly not the only spot. As with all of the city reservoirs where browns grow to large sizes, sawbellies provide the fuel and are the preferred bait for those who fish bait.

Fishermen take fewer very large browns here than in Pepacton. Four- to 6-pound brown trout are relatively common, but a fish of over 10 pounds will make more news here than in the Downsville area. Nonetheless, a few trout of 12 to 15 pounds are bested. While April and May and at least part of June are hopeful months for the Ashokan trout hunter, summer fishing for browns can take on a dead quality. Still, some regulars here speak of a good summertime rainbow bite, usually sometime from about late July through August. One biologist who has a boat here has done some stomach autopsies on these summer rainbows, and found young-of-the-year alewives. Perhaps there is a period during the summer when these small baitfish are especially available to the small-mouthed rainbows—let's say a concurrence of location within the reservoir.

There appear to be fewer large rainbow trout being taken by anglers in Ashokan, and New York State biologists have documented a decline in their growth rate, but it's unclear whether or not there are fewer of them. There are still huge numbers of wild rainbows in Esopus Creek and its tributaries, and since spawning-sized rainbows are nearly absent in the creek for most of the year (also documented), it's Ashokan rainbows that are making all those fingerlings. Still, on the wall of one bait shop near the reservoir, almost all the posted photographs are of browns.

In decades past, emerald shiners were abundant in Ashokan and were known to provide excellent forage for the rainbows, which often grew to 8 or 10 pounds. Back in those days, if you came here to fish for trout, you were primarily fishing for rainbows. There were no sawbellies, and large browns were probably uncommon. When emerald shiners declined and sawbellies appeared in the early 1970s (the events were probably related), the size of the rainbows went down. Rainbow trout, possibly due to their smaller mouths, do not seem to switch over to the sawbellies as early in their life cycle as do browns.

While browns are stocked in Ashokan, there are also wild fish that recruit back down from the Esopus and all its many fingers of contributory water. Rainbows are not stocked at all in Ashokan or in the Esopus. They are all wild fish. Rainbows born in the Esopus or its feeders migrate back down to the reservoir at one to two years of age. When they reach about 15 inches in length, they begin to reascend their river of birth for the goal of procreation. There is more on this in chapter 2.

There are very good numbers of self-sustaining smallmouth bass, and they receive probably as little pressure as do Pepacton's smallmouths. One noted spot for smallies is the east end of the east basin, where there are a lot of rock walls, ledges, and old quarries. In reality, there are probably dozens of spots in both basins where the habitat favors this hard-fighting game fish, and the time to locate them is when the water is drawn down.

Regulars here report taking largemouths, but they don't seem to be an important part of the mix. Similar to the situation on other of these deep reservoirs, the bucketmouths seem to be confined to the inner portions of some coves, where habitat may be somewhat more suitable.

This capacious and very deep reservoir was always well suited to the crepuscular and nocturnal walleye—then the sawbellies appeared. Walleye fry become part of the free-floating planktonic mass and apparently, the sawbellies—which feed on plankton—have been unkindly eating the walleye fry. From a sawbelly's viewpoint, this is preferable to having those fry grow big enough that the tables are turned. From a fisherman's point of view, there is one less excellent game fish in Ashokan to try for. One local bait shop owner termed walleyes "rare," although he sometimes sees as many as half a dozen on a good weekend. A state biologist used the term "relic population." But that same biologist reported having recently taken some extremely large specimens of 10 to 13 pounds during a netting survey.

Ashokan's east basin is much more subject to drawdowns than is the west basin. On the other hand, the east basin is considerably clearer; the west basin acts as a kind of "silt trap," settling out the turbidity of Esopus Creek.

Anglers coming to the east basin after early June really should have a thermometer, and they can often expect to find the thermocline unusually deep relative to some of the other reservoirs. This may help explain the difficulty of trout fishing after midseason.

Rondout

Completed during wartime in the 1940s, Rondout is, at 2,100 acres, a little bigger than Neversink. It's actually the deepest Catskill reservoir, the bottom being 180 feet down at one point. It's the most evenly shaped of the six reservoirs—essentially rectangular. It's 6 miles long and a mile or less wide, and sits at an elevation of about 875 feet. Game fish present are brown trout, lake trout, and smallmouth bass.

Rondout is the terminal end of tunnels from both Pepacton and Cannonsville Reservoirs, and in addition, water from Neversink Reservoir makes its way here via a discharge into Chestnut Creek. Water is frequently drawn off Rondout and makes its way via a tunnel into West Branch Reservoir in Putnam County. Because of all this moving water, one regular visitor here describes Rondout as more riverlike than lakelike. He adds that a true thermocline never sets up in summer and that the trout are more widely distributed but also sometimes harder to locate.

Brown trout have been stocked here for many years, and there is also some natural recruitment from tributary streams. Chestnut Creek, Trout Creek, and of course the upper Rondout River above the reservoir are all tributaries where spawning occurs. Still, Rondout is essentially tributary-poor compared to such impoundments as Pepacton, and the majority of browns taken are stocked fish. About 5,000 were planted in the most recent season. Seeforellen, a strain of brown trout that can grow very large, were also experimented with here. A couple of conquered fish of 19 to 20 pounds may have been Seeforellen; in any case, this European strain of *Salmo trutta* hasn't been stocked for a while now, and regular browns can grow to that size anyway.

The conservation department first planted lake trout here many years ago. This was a one-shot stocking of 40,000 surplus fall fingerlings. A few years later lakers started turning up in anglers' catches, and this inspired the regular stocking program that has continued to this day. Recently, a high percentage of lake trout recovered via netting by the DEC have been wild fish, showing that natural reproduction of lakers is now occurring. Still, about 7,500 were stocked this past season.

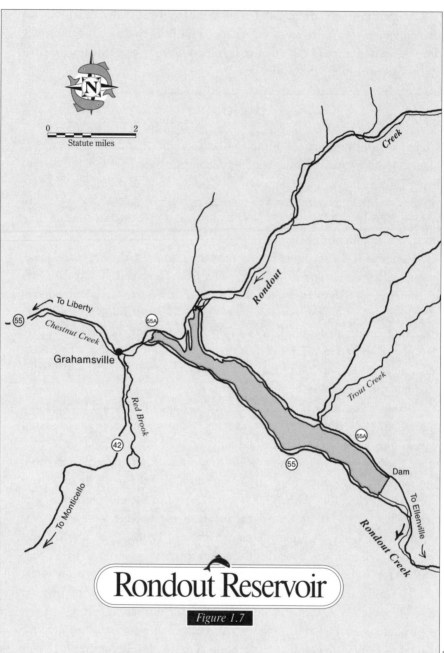

Statute miles

To Liberty

55

Chestnut Creek

Grahamsville

55A

Rondout

Creek

Red Brook

Trout Creek

42

55

55A

To Monticello

Dam

To Ellenville

Rondout Creek

Rondout Reservoir

Figure 1.7

Smallmouths are present but reportedly "not terribly abundant." Rondout has an unusually strong population of white suckers. There are carp, too.

A few landlocked salmon, at least as large as 12 pounds, have surprised Rondout sports. It is virtually certain that these fish made their way here through the tunnel from Neversink Reservoir.

In early spring both browns and lakers seem to migrate toward the west end of the reservoir, and many are taken at this time. Shore anglers do very well in those cold weeks of April, but boaters who drift sawbellies or troll lures also connect on both species. Because of this hot early-season action, as many as 300 fishermen's cars may be seen parked around the lake on a prime weekend in April. Thus, the lake hits a peak earlier than do some of the other reservoirs.

Later in spring the fish become harder to find. The cold-water-seeking lake trout go deep, and angler activity begins to center on the deeper east end, near the dam. Through late spring and even into summer, browns can be seen crashing through schools of sawbellies on the surface.

Return to Cannonsville

Last night I dreamed I was back in Cannonsville. Imagine. It isn't the first time I had that dream. I dreamed it a lot of times since we left, but I thought I was all over it by now. Sometimes I think I will never forget, though it has been how many years?

I was sixteen when it all started. Seems like only such a short time instead of twenty some years. I used to go with Daddy to the creamery in the old Dodge every morning. I loved to load the empty milk cans on the truck as they came back out after being washed. Dad would go in the creamery and I'd have the cans all loaded and tied up when he came out.

Then one morning George Pepper was telling all the farmers he heard they were going to dam up the West Branch and make it a reservoir like they did at Pepacton a few years back. We laughed. George was a great one for spreading rumors, always getting excited over nothing. But this wasn't nothing, it was something, and things moved fast after that terrible morning that changed all our lives.

First the surveyors, then the lawyers, the politicians, the appraisers. Suddenly the valley was full of strange people in fancy clothes everywhere, in Mr. Nelson's store, in the post office, in the street. And there were official notices on the telephones explaining that New York City was taking our farms in order to increase their water supply.

I guess if anybody had thought about it they would have figured out that someday it would happen. Our long, narrow valley with the Delaware rolling down through the middle, high hills on both sides, just a perfect spot to dam the river, and close enough to New York City to be piped down there, but nobody ever thought about it.

I remember the happy times along that old river, daddy plowing the long meadow in the spring and brother Jim and I fishing and swimming in that lovely water. And the happy times we had at the Grange, and in the church, where we used to go every Sunday, the picnics, strawberry festivals, Halloween parties, something always happening. We were such a happy family, but I guess you never know till it's gone.

Mom refused to listen to any talk about the dam at all. "I don't want to hear about the damn dam," she used to say. Mom was born on the farm and dad worked for grandpa and finally married mom, so ma was really the boss about things like that. She said nobody was going to take her farm away and she would get the shotgun and chase them off if she had to. But when the appraisers came with papers to sign, mom ran upstairs and locked herself in the bedroom and bawled like I never heard her before. I didn't think mom ever cried, but she sure let it out that day.

"Mr. Hanson, I think we have been very fair with you, we have given you every dollar your farm is worth."

Dad looked up the stairs to where mom was locked in the bedroom and said, "How much do you pay for a broken heart?"

Things happened fast after that, auctions all around, our beautiful herd of Holsteins sold for almost nothing. There were so many people selling out, and butchers jamming our pet cows with electric prods to load them in their trucks. I ran behind the barn and cried worse than mom and that was the night daddy had his heart attack and he was dead in a week, and we couldn't even bury him in our local churchyard where all our people were buried. They had to take him clear to Walton to some strange cemetery I never saw before, because the church was being torn down and the graves had to be moved.

Well, mom moved to Deposit to an apartment over a store. Imagine, after her whole life on the farm, being cooped up in an apartment. Jim got a job in Pennsylvania, and I hardly ever see him. And me, I married Eddie Mancini, they had the farm just below us on the river, and his folks and ours used to change work year after year. I guess that's how we fell in love, working in the haymow in the big red barn, and sometimes when nobody was around we would forget about mowing and be making out in the back mow. Jim caught us once but he never told.

We moved to Delhi and Eddie got a job on the farm but he finally went to work in the college. It is a pretty good job, but sometimes we'd give anything to be down in Cannonsville Valley. I just wish I could stop dreaming about it.

Note: In New York City's process of creating six water-supply reservoirs in the Catskill Mountains, dozens of villages and thousands of people were displaced, many never to be reoriented. We are honored to be able to reprint this essay, which first appeared, anonymously, in *Catskill Country* magazine. Reprinted with permission.

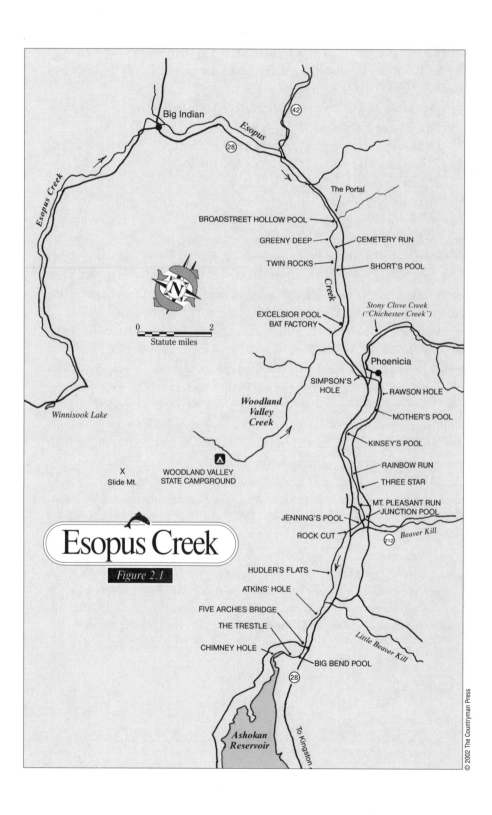

Big Indian

42

Esopus

28

The Portal

BROADSTREET HOLLOW POOL

GREENY DEEP — CEMETERY RUN

TWIN ROCKS — SHORT'S POOL

Creek

EXCELSIOR POOL
BAT FACTORY

Stony Clove Creek
("Chichester Creek")

Phoenicia

SIMPSON'S
HOLE

RAWSON HOLE

Woodland
Valley
Creek

MOTHER'S POOL

Winnisook Lake

KINSEY'S POOL

RAINBOW RUN

THREE STAR

▲

WOODLAND VALLEY
STATE CAMPGROUND

MT. PLEASANT RUN
JUNCTION POOL

X
Slide Mt.

JENNING'S POOL

ROCK CUT

212 Beaver Kill

0   2
Statute miles

Esopus Creek opus Creek

Figure 2.1

HUDLER'S FLATS

ATKINS' HOLE

FIVE ARCHES BRIDGE

THE TRESTLE

CHIMNEY HOLE

BIG BEND POOL

Little Beaver Kill

28

Esopus Creek

To Kingston

Ashokan
Reservoir

CHAPTER 2

The Esopus

Esopus Creek contains one of the best wild rainbow trout populations in the Northeast. Like the Neversink, it is born on Slide Mountain, the Catskills' highest peak at 4,201 feet. Unlike the Neversink, the Esopus often has a chalky look, a result of pockets of the clay that also lends a bit of chalkiness to certain other Catskill rivers.

The true beginning of Esopus Creek is often said to be Winnisook Lake at 2,800 feet, although the river's drainage extends higher into the mountains. It flows essentially north from that source to the hamlet of Big Indian, and then turns and heads east, then southeast, to Ashokan Reservoir. Above Big Indian, access is from Big Indian Road. Below Big Indian, access is essentially from Route 28, from the local road parallel to Route 28, or from side streets or pull-offs from either of these. Although there is some posting, access below Big Indian is very good. Some of this stems from the fact that private landowners have generously left the riverbanks open to fishermen; in addition, the river is right next to the road and is thus located within the state's easement along that road. There are also about 8.8 bank miles of DEC-secured easements for anglers. From the Five Arches bridge downstream a mile or so to the fabled Chimney Hole, and beyond this to the reservoir, it is New York City watershed property. This is open to the public, but a free watershed permit is technically needed.

More so than any other major Catskill river, this is a fast, tumbling, pocket-water stream. The classic, riffle-pool character of streams like the Beaver Kill is replaced here with pools that are rockier, faster, less distinct, often shorter, and usually less kind to the dry fly. In truth, the Esopus with its great head of fish is often difficult, and that may partially be because there just aren't that many good pocket-water fishermen. It is not restful fishing. You have to grab a trout from here and another from there, as the river flows ceaselessly by. The answer here is not one big mystery locked into the depths of a dark, brooding pool. For every hour of fishing it is a hundred mysteries, one for each piece of whitewater that sucks your dry fly down, pulls your nymph or streamer up, or wedges your bait or lure into some hopeless crevice.

As you'll see in subsequent chapters, many Catskill rivers break down for one reason or another into distinct sections. Nowhere is that more true than on the Esopus, with the real line of demarcation being the "portal" above Phoenicia. But before I talk more about the different sections of the Esopus, let me first set the backdrop for this very important Catskill river.

The Esopus contains brook, brown, and rainbow trout, but rainbows are easily the most abundant. The 'bows exist in the main river, of course, but there are also "tons of fingerling rainbows in most of the tributaries" according to one biologist. Brookies are mainly restricted to the headwaters just below Winnisook Lake and to the tributary streams. From above (upstream of) Route 28 at Big Indian all the way down to Ashokan Reservoir, browns and rainbows mix. Here, in addition to large numbers of wild rainbows and smaller numbers of wild browns, some 22,000 hatchery-reared brown trout are stocked annually. In the most recent season, this included 2,000 two-year-old fish of 14 inches. These hatchery fish, although far less numerous than their wild counterparts, are much easier to catch than the fish of wild origin, and they account for a disproportionate part of the catch in the early season. Holdover of these stocked browns is poor, and in fact by late season, they figure far less heavily in the catch. Creel surveys show that over the course of the whole season, about 87 percent of the fish caught are of wild origin.

The DEC has done some recent sampling of the Esopus trout population, and the figures it provided me with are lower than the estimates I received for earlier editions of this book. Even with these new figures, though, it's clear that the Esopus still contains a remarkable trout population.

While it's difficult to accurately assess a river as large as the Esopus, biologists project that it has a standing crop of about 11,000 trout from Big Indian down to the portal at Allaben, and another 60,000 trout from the portal down to the reservoir. (There is a pretty big plus or minus factor here.) If you did some fast figuring, you would see that this equates to about 28 trout every 10 yards! One-year-old-and-better fish make up about 60 percent of the overall crop, and among these, some 95 percent are wild. Rainbows dominate the wild segment, but there are very respectable numbers of wild browns, too. Other than parts of the Delaware, no major Catskill river can boast a higher percentage of wild trout. Indeed, few large rivers in the Northeast offer such good wild-trout fishing.

Almost all of the nonspawning rainbows taken in the Esopus are smaller than 11 inches, and a big percentage of them fall into the 8- to 9-inch range. That's because most rainbows migrate down to Ashokan Reservoir at one to two years of age. Happily, though, when these AWOL trout get up to about 15 inches, they start to come back up from the lake to spawn. The famous Esopus "spawning rainbows" are not easy to catch, but they have made for good fishing stories for decades. One of those stories appeared in the writings of A. J. McClane. An icon to serious young fishermen of my generation, McClane—presumably sometime in the 1940s—stalked and conquered a spawner of 6 pounds, as weighed on the scales of the old Folkert Store in Phoenicia (this venerable establishment remained in the Folkert family until just five years ago). As discussed in the previous chapter, rainbows are not growing as large in Ashokan as they did in the past. Thus, while the average spawning rainbows taken by anglers may still be about 15 to 20 inches, the larger ones of bygone days are seen much less often.

The run appears to occur primarily between late February and late April, with the peak of the activity possibly occurring before the April 1 opener in some years. Nonetheless, large rainbows, possibly spent spawners, are sometimes observed in the river as late as about early June. One Esopus regular believes that there is a second wave of lake-run rainbows in June. He describes these as smaller fish, about 14 to 16 inches.

In midautumn some large rainbows and browns ascend from Ashokan Reservoir and are taken occasionally by anglers. Browns spawn in fall, so that makes sense. Do the rainbows come up the river in autumn to dine on brown trout eggs, just as large browns run up Lake Ontario feeders to feast on salmon eggs? Rainbows are known to spawn as early as January, so another theory could be that the autumn specimens are the vanguard of that run. In any case, mid-October to mid-November is the best part of autumn if you want to try for an oversized lake-run fish.

With the great number of wild rainbows present in the Esopus, you

There is no shortage of rock on the Esopus. Spin-fishermen who become frustrated fishing bait on the bottom might consider switching to spinners or salted minnows.

might wonder why browns are stocked at all. As one official told me, "We stock here because we've always stocked." What he meant was that the public is so convinced of the idea that you have to stock trout to have them in the river that stocking has become almost automatic, even in rivers that have plenty of wild fish. Personally, I'd rather fish for wild trout, and when I'm not working on books like this I tend to fish in places where there are only wild trout. But even if many state officials have the same overall feelings on the subject (they do), the politics of stocking are very ingrained. When an explanation is needed of why browns are stocked in the Esopus at all, it goes something like this: "The hatchery fish are much easier to catch, as proven repeatedly by creel surveys." This is true, and in fact in early season, the stocked browns constitute a majority of the catch. Moreover, it's argued that the hatchery browns are a little bigger on average than the rainbows, making for additional angler satisfaction. The chunky two-year-old fish that the department now stocks put additional weight behind this argument.

There are three fairly distinct sections to the Esopus. Let's look at the characteristics of each.

Section 1 is from Winnisook Lake down to the village of Big Indian. In the extreme upper part of this 7-mile stretch, the Esopus touches a little state land, and that makes for public access. Up here, there are bright little native brook trout. Regrettably, from above the slow-motion hamlet of Oliverea all the way down to Big Indian, the Esopus tumbles through private land, some of which is ferociously posted (PATROLLED!—POLICE PATROLLED!—REWARD!). Still, there is public easement on some of the water between Route 28 and Lost Clove Road. There once were some nice pools here, but like many Catskill streams this section was rearranged by the 1996 January flood. Park in the big lot at Route 28 or by Lost Clove Road and take a look for yourself. In spring it's often very nice, although as the season advances this water thins out rather rapidly.

For many people, the Esopus really begins at Big Indian. Here it picks up steam considerably as it absorbs Birch Creek, where beavers have been hard at work. Birch is another one of several dozen smallish to midsized streams in the Catskills that big-trout-smitten anglers of the new generation almost completely avoid. If you'd like to take a poke at it, head west on Route 28 from Big Indian and take the first left turn down to the brook. An abandoned railroad bed may abet access, but watch out for posted signs, which are intermittent the length of the brook.

To return to the Esopus, I'll call the water from Big Indian down to the portal at Allaben (not even a dot on the map) section 2. It's 5 miles in length.

This pleasant but still fairly small reach of the Esopus varies from about 30 to 40 feet wide and 1 to 3 feet deep, and the upper part of it is nicely shaded. Although it's paralleled closely by Route 28, it still has a bit of a feeling of wildness to it. When it's at a normal height, there are charming if small pools stitched together by fast riffles, glides, and plenty of pocket water. Access is quite good. You can park at the special fishermen's parking area at Big Indian mentioned just above, and fish downstream. If you were to drive the country road that parallels the stream on its north side between Route 42 and Big Indian, you'd see two anglers' parking areas and some very pretty water. There are established Department of Transportation (DOT) pull-offs on Route 28 at several points along the Esopus both above and below the portal. Some of these are located between Big Indian and Shandaken. Another is near Peck Hollow. Still another is just upstream of Mount Pleasant. Generally speaking, parking is not a problem for the Esopus angler.

As opposed to the part of the river below the portal, the flows in this section are all natural. If it rains, it's up. If it doesn't, it's down. The entire Esopus Valley is subject to severe flooding, and the past decade has seen some ferocious floods. But when a dry spell sets in, section 2 can become low and unappealing. Another problem here is this: When the lower river is turbid due to heavy inflows from the portal and/or heavy sediment washed in from certain tributaries, most anglers head up here to find clearer water. When this happens, section 2 can get very crowded, so much so that I often hop over the mountain to the upper East Branch of the Delaware (see chapter 7).

Section 2 offers up plenty of browns and rainbows, and even a spawning rainbow in-season. It's been seen that the spring spawners ascend the river even beyond Big Indian, so in spring you can tie into one of those red-flanked bruisers even up here.

But the fish you'll most often catch will be wild rainbows averaging 7 to 9 inches, and stocked browns—as well as some holdovers—averaging perhaps 9 to 11 inches. State biologists note that there are relatively few browns in the catch after mid-July, but with the two-year-old fish now being stocked, there is at least a greater chance of hooking up with one large enough to put a bend into your rod.

Since I am not intimately familiar with the Esopus, for the following hatch information I relied in large part on Hank Rope of Big Indian Guide Service. This would apply to the entire river, although Hank thinks the hatches are poorer below the portal, and that—more broadly speaking—some sections of the river seem to consistently have more bugs than others.

While insect hatches on the Esopus are not as heavy or diverse as on the Beaver Kill–Delaware system, there are still some good ones. One of the best is the blue-winged olive (several darkish mayfly species), which can occur in any month of the year. They seem to be larger—up to size 14—early and late in the season, and smaller—size 18 to 22—during the warmer months of summer. As soon as the water hits about 52 degrees Fahrenheit in spring, trout may rise to them. In fall, trout may come up for these and other flies at a lower water temperature, even down to about 45 degrees. This curiosity may be another of the several reasons why knowledgeable anglers like autumn fishing on the Esopus.

The popular *Isonychias,* both a common name and a generic name for two or three large, darkish mayfly species, constitute another important hatch, as mentioned elsewhere in this chapter. They may be seen anytime from late May to September, and when they are present, a Leadwing Coachman wet fly can be very effective.

The Hendricksons that can sometimes hatch in great numbers on other Catskill rivers have a definite presence here. The last week of April is the time to be looking for them. Perhaps a month later, scattered numbers of March browns and gray foxes, two related mayfly species in the genus *Stenonema*, may be seen over Esopus currents.

Stoneflies of several species and sizes hatch over a broad part of the first half of the trout season. Early on, anglers sometimes observe fairly small numbers of early brown stones, while in June and July larger stoneflies hatch, often in the evening or early morning. One tactic for fishing this hatch is to fish a buggy fly like a Muddler or Woolly Bugger in the shallows late in the afternoon as the light starts to fade.

The warm weather that sets in in June brings the promise of more than just large stoneflies. From late June through early September light Cahills may be seen, especially toward dark. These large yellowish mayflies (a few different species) are usually best imitated with a size 14 dry fly, but have along some 12s, too. Another light-colored, almost whitish mayfly that can occur from late spring into summer is the *Potamanthus*, usually best imitated by a size 10 to 12 dry.

Terrestrials can be important on this river. For example, in late August there is often a showing of black ants. While the Esopus has excellent populations of minnows, such as black-nosed dace, few anglers really have the skill necessary to take fish consistently with streamers and bucktails. A good time to try these traditional tempters of larger trout is fall, when some bigger fish are in the river.

The mileage I've just discussed is often called the "natural Esopus." Well, at Allaben the famous and sometimes infamous portal turns it into an unnatural river. But first, what is the portal?

It is the terminus of New York City's 18.5-mile Shandaken Tunnel, which delivers water underground from near the bottom of Schoharie Reservoir located to the north of the Esopus drainage. Constructed in 1924, the tunnel serves to divert water from the Schoharie River drainage—whose waters would otherwise be "lost" to the Mohawk River and eventually the sea—to Ashokan Reservoir via the Esopus. This great though intermittent inflow of sometimes cold and often turbid water has a major impact on section 3 of the Esopus, that portion from the portal down to the reservoir (about 12 miles).

Thanks to the efforts of both public agencies and private conservation groups, water releases via the portal are now more controlled in an attempt to bring better fisheries management to the Esopus. Thus, Esopus flows below the portal do not fluctuate as drastically as they once did. Nonetheless, there are many individuals and advocacy groups who believe that portal waters are more turbid than in decades past, as a result of greater turbidity in Schoharie Reservoir. Why is the reservoir more turbid? Strata of clay exist at at least two elevations in the Catskills, and very heavy rains can open up what are called "lenses" of clay. This happened noticeably during the January 1996 flood on the West Kill, a tributary to Schoharie Reservoir. Not only was the West Kill badly eroded, but Schoharie Reservoir remained turbid that entire year—clay does not easily settle out. Those ardent about Esopus fly-fishing believe that what they see as greater turbidity below the portal has hurt the insect life, and possibly the spawning habitat. There is litigation pending in this matter.

As policy now stands, there are up to four especially heavy "recreational releases" made between June and early October. These are for the canoeists, kayakers, and tubers who also use the river a great deal in summer, and they can be on the order of 1,000 cubic feet per second. These releases and the heavy recreational use associated with them can make section 3 all but unfishable. Still, there is some evidence that such a big release will bring large browns up from the reservoir, especially in September and October. These larger trout apparently remain in the river for at least a few days, so that when the water level subsides, the stage has been set for some good fishing. In October, browns intent on spawning may stay much longer after being magnetized by the heavy pulse of water.

Despite the high roily water the portal often creates, biologists believe that it does more good than harm. The water from the reservoir is fairly cold, generally 50 to 60 degrees Fahrenheit at the portal (although sometimes lower or higher), and in summer this cools off the lower river, making it a quasi-tailwater stream. As long as the flows aren't too heavy or murky, the large volume of water makes for more pleasant fishing, especially from late spring through summer. In fact, conditions are often ideal, and the trout perky although not always easy to catch.

Just below the portal the stream averages 70 to 90 feet in width and 2 to 4 feet in depth. The pools are a little bigger here, though still quite short by Catskill river standards. As you head farther downriver to Phoenicia, Mount Tremper, and beyond, the river grows considerably thanks to such significant tributaries as Woodland Valley Creek, Chichester Creek, the Beaver Kill, and others. Now the river begins to average 90 to 120 feet wide, and there are places where it's over your head.

From the portal down to the Five Arches bridge, access is where you find it. The actual banks of the stream are not highly developed, but human activities all along the Route 28 corridor increase each season. There are guaranteed state access areas along section 3, and there are even a few fishermen's parking areas that are reasonably easy to spot from Route 28. If you look at the map, you'll see that just below the portal the river pulls a bit away from the road for a few miles. This nice section is backed up on the western side by rugged forest preserve lands, and it's worth trying to find access to.

To my mind, the reason to visit Esopus Creek is to fish big water. Given that bent, the best of the Esopus is from the bridge at Mount Tremper, immediately above the point where Route 212 jogs off toward Woodstock, down to the reservoir. One point of access is just opposite Hudler Road. There's a bus garage here and if you pull behind the garage—tell them you're fishing, if they ask—you'll see a dirt road heading down toward the stream. With a car you can go partway; with a four-wheel drive, a little farther. In either case, it will be just a short walk down to some of the nicest-looking water on the river. When I visited this section on August 1, there were large numbers of stonefly nymph cases on the rocks, and I watched a mink making its rounds on the rugged, undeveloped far bank. Small rainbows were in active mode due to the strong, cool infusions from the portal that day.

To fish the wide, engrossing water below the Five Arches bridge, park in the several spaces just west of the bridge. Then just walk the abandoned railroad tracks or the river downstream. At this point, a walk of half an hour or less would get you to the reservoir. Below the old train bridge, the tallest peaks in the Catskills stand as a dramatic backdrop. This is quite possibly the most beautiful big water in the Catskills. Stay off the bridge itself, which is decrepit and dangerous, but do fish the deep pockets around the bridge. And of course, do wet a line in the famous Chimney Hole, a large and magnificent pool just up from the reservoir.

The lower part of section 3 is big water, and heavy portal releases and/or heavy rains can make this section bullish and unwadable. On the other hand, below Phoenicia fly-casting conditions become increasingly favorable since the river is large and open. Sometimes too open, with the sun baking the river and its channel.

What of services in this valley? There are a few bait and tackle and sport shops along Route 28 as you head northwest from Kingston. There is also a shop in Phoenicia, the largest village on the river. Motels and eating places along Route 28 and in Phoenicia are numerous, and several of the restaurants are quite interesting and nice. One place to camp is the Woodland Valley State Campground, located on Woodland Valley Creek, an important Esopus tributary with its own alluring pools and riffles.

In sync with most other Catskill rivers, the fly-rod is increasingly the weapon of choice, but spin-fishermen skilled at working blade spinners through this fast water can do extremely well.

It's often said that bait- and spin-fishermen have the big advantage in spring. I really don't agree with this old cliché. In early spring trout are relatively inactive and are more difficult to take by any method. Conversely, when water temperatures approach the optimal range for trout—high 50s to low 60s—trout are easier to take by all methods. This applies in any trout water. In the Catskill region, these ideal stream temperatures usually occur from late May to mid-June. Of course on the Esopus, this projection is greatly complicated by the inflows from the portal. The extent of the releases and where you're fishing in relation to the portal will affect the stream temperatures. Nevertheless, if you fish from late May to mid-June, you may experience some of the best fishing of the year. Naturally, if a good hatch comes off when the water is 52 degrees or, at the other end, 68 degrees, you can have a banner day regardless of the time of year. By the same token, a heavy rain after a dry spell, especially between mid-June and early August, can spell superb bait- or lure-fishing. The point of all this is, if you're trying to decide what method to use, there is more to the equation than just "bait early in the season, flies later in the season."

In early June, in particular, I find that spinner-fishing can be outstanding. My favorite spinner is the size 1 Mepps with a blade that's silver on one side and red/white on the other. Worked effectively and skillfully through the pocket water, this genre of lure is the ticket here. If you're catching lots of fish you elect to return, it's very important to cut off or bend down two of the three hooks on the treble. It will make release of the fish much easier. By the way, the biggest fish I've taken on lures here were browns, and most of them fell for a 2¾-inch Rapala worked through the slower runs. Gold lures will catch more browns, silver more rainbows. If you don't believe that, try it and see for yourself.

I think you have to be masochistic to fish worms on this very rocky stream, since you'll be stuck constantly. Live or salted minnows are popular here, however, and usually account for the biggest browns taken each year.

*Fly casting on the big Esopus water between the Five Arches bridge
and the reservoir. Just a hundred yards or so below this is the
fabled Chimney Hole, where a state record brown trout was once caught.
All this pocket water is flush with small wild rainbows, but large spawners
from the reservoir are possible at certain times.*

Over the years, more than a few browns of better than 5 pounds have discovered a hook in a minnow tossed their way. Cloudy, misty, rainy days are
perfect for this tactic. Even when you're fly-fishing, those kinds of days are
usually more fruitful than bright, sunny days.

Some say the Esopus is a wet-fly stream. I would rephrase this to say that
dry-fly fishing is fruitful on this river less often than on some other major
Catskill rivers. Fishing a dry in fast water is always challenging, and besides
that the hatches are, as already mentioned, not as abundant as on some other
Catskill streams. Most likely, above the portal is where hatching timetables
are the most normal. Below the portal, the colder temperatures and unnatural flows make for less predictable hatching.

Wets and nymphs worked patiently and methodically will serve the fly-
fisherman well. It's silly to list "the best patterns." If you're from the "impres-
sionistic school," you'll carry a few different wets and nymphs and do well if
you're good. If you're from the "exact imitation school," you'll carry dozens
or hundreds of patterns and you'll also do well, again if you're a good fisherman. I recommend you try a sinking-tip line, though. You'll struggle a lot

less keeping those subsurface flies down where they should be much of the time. Also, keep your casts short! These tips are most important in early season when the trout will be sluggish and very, very closely attached to the bottom of the stream.

The trout season on the Esopus runs from April 1 through November 30. Not only does midautumn give you a chance at a large brown or rainbow from the reservoir, but it also offers at least a fair shot at a good hatch. I have encountered some very good hatches throughout the month of September and into early October. *Isonychia* and small to medium-sized blue-winged olives are the bugs I've most often seen on these late-season forays.

The Catskill Fishing in Print

Fortunately for all of us, some of the eulogies sung for the Catskills have been set down in print. There is an increasing number of fishing books just about the Catskills, and there are also innumerable books with sections on Catskill fishing. Further, this mountain region has served as an ongoing laboratory for fly-fishers *de plume,* who have incorporated many a Catskill episode into their broader guidebooks.

A well-researched and well-written treatise is *Catskill Rivers,* by Austin Francis. It traces the history of the major Catskill rivers from the time European settlers arrived. The early railroads, logging on the Delaware, the gruesome effects of the tanning and wood chemical industries—all these early river activities are couched in the scholarly and effective prose of Mr. Francis. A newer book by Mr. Francis is *Land of Little Rivers: A Story in Photos of Catskill Fly Fishing,* a lavish coffee table book that will extract an even hundred dollars from your wallet. Incorporating parts of *Catskill Rivers,* this more ambitious enterprise features some superb color photographs by Enrico Ferorelli. These are so important to the book that one wonders why Mr. Ferorelli wasn't given a cover credit. In any case, while the "great camps" of the Adirondacks from the Gilded Age have been well chronicled, the private fishing clubs of the Catskills have remained generally hidden from the eyes of the public. *Land of Little Rivers* brings these clubs, and their colorful characters, into the light of day.

Books have started to appear on individual Catskill rivers. One is *Beaverkill: The History of a River and Its People.* It's always reassuring to know that when someone writes a history of a trout river, he has put in lots of hard fishing time on it. Ed Van Put is not only a professional fisheries technician but an ardent fly-fisher, and he knows the Beaver Kill and the entire Delaware River system like few others; he's the one that other Catskill writers go to for their information. In *Beaverkill* he presents a wealth of information about this renowned stream and its tributaries, in a style both perspicuous and welcoming.

Leonard M. Wright, Jr., who helped to bring attention to the importance of caddisflies with his highly regarded earlier books, including *Fishing the Dry Fly as a Living Insect* (no doubt based heavily on Catskill experiences), has written a book on the Neversink River titled *Neversink*. This is neither a historical book nor a guidebook, but a personal investigation of a single body of water. Being privileged enough to fish on Edward Ringwood Hewitt's golden water, Wright seems to have been smitten with Hewitt's proclivity for physically manipulating trout streams. This is only a symptom, of course, but it speaks volumes, and so in *Neversink*—as in so many contemporary fly-fishing books that probe—any hope of "understanding a trout stream" is condemned to failure by a lack of fundamental understanding.

Fishless Days, Angling Nights is a collection of some two dozen short stories and reminiscences about fishing and the outdoors, set mainly in the 1930s, '40s, and '50s. Some of the stories are better than others, but the best are superb. Although outdoor locales in the Adirondacks, Pennsylvania, and even suburban New York City are referenced, the book is more about the Catskills than anywhere else. Those days—and nights—were golden for author Sparse Grey Hackle and his cronies, who passed the halcyon days in pleasant misery at the bar of the Antrim Lodge (and even, occasionally, on the banks of the Beaver Kill). Just one story, "The Lotus Eaters," is worth the price of the book. It centers on an old fishing club located on the upper Beaver Kill, of which Sparse was a member. Decorated only with whiskey bottles, a kerosene lamp, and a "grocery store calendar for the year 1910," the "clubhouse" makes a Buddhist monastery seem like Versailles. Hopelessly satisfied with their little bit of nirvana along the timeless Beaver Kill, the 20-odd members are passionate only in their abject fear of change in any form or manner. This story could only have been written by the late Sparse, who was once nearly ejected from the club for attempting to move the 1910 calendar (presumably sometime around 1940).

One of the most famous fly-tiers in the world was Harry Darbee, who left behind not only six or seven decades' worth of fishing, drinking, and raising holy hell with the good-for-nothing road builders, but also a fine book: *Catskill Fly Tier: My Life, Times and Techniques* (coauthored with

Austin Francis). More than just a valuable reference for fly-tiers, who will pick up many of Harry's innovative ideas, it's also a good full jigger's worth of classic Catskill memorabilia. Lest I be excoriated, let me add that Harry's wife, Elsie, was equally renowned as a tier of trout flies, and an equal half of the Darbee team. She always greeted me with a smile and a warm welcome in that crowded little house that was one of the foci of the fly-fishing world.

Walt and Winnie Dette were the other famous Roscoe-area fly-tiers, and they too have been honored with a book. *The Dettes—A Catskill Legend* was penned by the gentlemanly and well-published Eric Leiser, author of many important fly-fishing books.

The distinguished founder of *Esquire* magazine, Arnold Gingrich, wrote several good books about fishing. Two that are well infused with the Catskills are *The Well Tempered Angler* and *The Joys of Trout*.

For the more pragmatic, *A Book of Trout Flies* is truly one of the pioneering books in the literature of fly-fishing. Written, of course, by Preston Jennings, this book was first published in 1935 and it remains relevant today. Specific references to Catskill hatches are numerous.

New Streamside Guide to Naturals and Their Imitations, by Art Flick, is part of the backbone of fly-fishing literature, and is one of the best-selling fishing books of all time. Research for it was done primarily in the Catskills, and so the timetables and patterns are especially relevant.

In his little book *Remembrances of Rivers Past,* Ernest Schwiebert has a very nice chapter titled "Song of the Catskills." It is heady stuff of olden days, a cook's tour of waters large and small, drawn from Schwiebert's prodigious catalog of experiences. Some of today's writing teams who churn out the most popular hatch-oriented fishing guidebooks ought to look here, to see that fly-fishing is about much more than just science. (By the way, if you can't find *Remembrances,* look for the more recently issued *The Complete Schwiebert.)*

There are many, many more books that discuss fishing in the Catskills. Only a few of these are *Seventy Five Years a Trout and Salmon Fisherman* by Edward Ringwood Hewitt; *How to Take Trout on Wet Flies and Nymphs* and *The Trout and the Fly,* both by Ray Ovington; *The Dry Fly and Fast Water* by George M. LaBranche; *The Compleat Brown Trout* by Cecil Heacox; and *The Notes and Letters of Theodore Gordon,* edited by John McDonald.

If you find yourself in the Esopus Creek area, stop at the Phoenica Library on Main Street and spend a little time in the upstairs angler's reading room. You'll find a great collection of fly-fishing books, including all the important Catskill titles.

CHAPTER 3

The Neversink
and Schoharie

In the deepest, most remote part of the Catskill Mountains, a minute
trickle drip-drips like a broken kitchen faucet. Its sound completely
muffled by a spongy carpet of moss, the headwater brook only slowly
gains strength as it makes its way down Balsam Cap Mountain. When finally it does form a pool, it is still far above where any brook trout could live.
But at any given time, this little holding pen of water might be visited by
black bear, deer, coyote, bobcat, or fisher. As the wind whistles across Friday,
Balsam, and Table Top, it's the only sound to be heard. Set in the middle of
some 200,000 acres of forever-wild state land, nothing unnatural, not even
the roar of a faraway truck, can be heard.

I have backpacked for trout far up the East Branch Neversink and deer
hunted even farther upstream, beyond the permanent river and up the little
feeder brook just described. I have also explored the lower mileage above
where the Neversink meets the Basher Kill, several miles upstream of where
the conjoined waters merge with the Delaware River at Port Jervis. I have
fished in between, too, although sadly, much of this middle mileage is posted
or impounded.

There are two branches of the upper Neversink, and the Catskills'
highest peak—Slide—is mother to both of them. The West Branch gathers

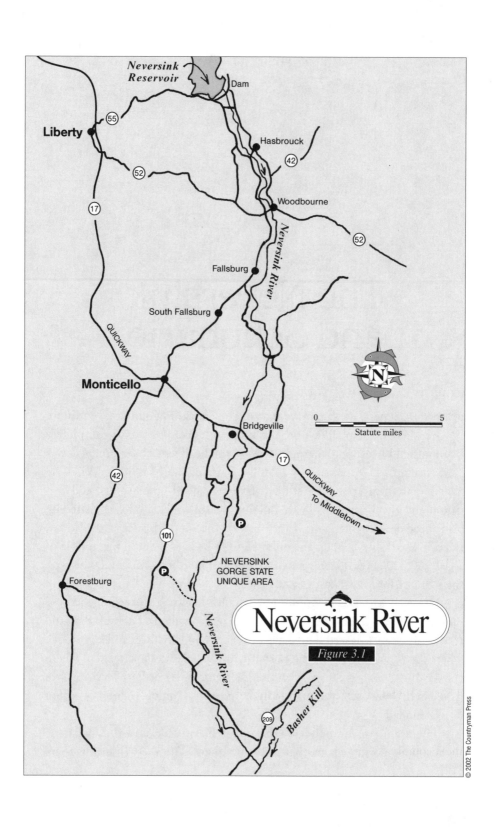

Neversink River

Figure 3.1

itself as it flows west off Slide, and then turns to the southwest as it parallels County Route 1. Just east of Round Pond, which through its outlet sends in a little water, the West Branch heads south and joins the East Branch some 2 miles later at Claryville. All in all, the West Branch cuts a 22-mile scratch in these cool, shady, central Catskills.

In its upper mileage just southwest of Winnisook Lake, the West Branch does bisect a little state land, and while the water is very small here, there still are brook trout. I verified this on a hike during telling late-summer conditions. In fact, I was rather amazed to see a 7-inch brookie dart for cover in a tiny pool only slightly south of Winnisook. This is the extreme headwaters of the West Branch. Below this there is little state land, and so the best chance for public access is at the Frost Valley YMCA.

There are three ways to fish Frost Valley's 2.5 miles of the upper West Branch. First, if you stay at the camp as a registered guest—the camp is open to the public autumn, winter, and spring but closed summer because of youth camps—you may fish not only the main stream, but also several small but sometimes productive little tributaries on the camp property: Pigeon Brook and Biscuit Brook are two of these. There are also a couple of stocked ponds on the Frost Valley property, and on one of these, Lake Cole, ice fishing is permitted.

To be able to fish here at any time during open fishing season, April 1 through October 15, you will have to apply for membership in the Frost Valley Fly Fishers. Dues are currently $125 per year, and you must be interviewed by personnel at Frost Valley. At the time of this writing, there were openings, but call Frost Valley to check. Note that all people fishing the Frost Valley mileage must fish with flies only, and there are special restrictions on take limits, too. Spin-fishing is allowed on Lake Cole.

Finally, a guest of a club member can buy a day pass for $15 but is entitled to fish here just once a year.

Frost Valley club members fishing the river have reported taking brookies up to 15 or 16 inches, and a few browns are also present. In the season just passed, club diaries show that the brook trout caught averaged 6 to 9 inches, with the largest one going 14 inches (caught in one of the tributaries!).

Frost Valley has recently begun offering fly-fishing programs for adults. That would be something else to look into.

Downstream of Frost Valley the West Branch is again tightly posted.

The equally pristine and scenic East Branch of the Neversink is also almost completely private along its most tempting section. You must head far upstream, to the Denning lean-to, before state forest preserve land frees the East Branch for public use.

Downstream of Claryville, the main branch Neversink is comprised of some of the most famous trout water in the world. Here the ghosts of no less than Edward Ringwood Hewitt and Theodore Gordon haunt the sparkling currents where they once fished. But even if you believe in ghosts, the chance of your ever seeing their apparitions is about nil. This prime trout water is in private hands and is very tightly posted. The well connected who do fish here sometimes report seeing salmon parr, or even mature salmon moving up from the reservoir.

That New York City water-supply reservoir, Neversink, inundated 7.2 miles of the Neversink River in 1955. No one will ever again wade this once-glorious water, but angling from a boat is there for those who want it. Chapter 1 introduces this possibility to you.

From the dam at Neversink Reservoir downstream to the Neversink Gorge (see below), the Neversink today offers some good trout fishing. This is thanks to cold water released in modest amounts from the reservoir, and also to the public fishing rights that the DEC has worked so hard to obtain. The New Paltz office of the DEC (see page 211) offers a free map that shows in detail where these easements are located. Ask for the "Neversink River Public Fishing Rights Map."

By the time the Neversink has reached the Route 17 Quickway bridge, the effect of the cold releases has diminished, and higher-than-desirable temperatures can occur in summer. Still, more than a few trout are caught in this segment just above and below Bridgeville, and angling pressure—extremely light the length of the river compared to the Beaver Kill or Delaware—is probably minimal. In any case, below the hamlet of Bridgeville the Neversink River falls into a steep gorge. In this shady, rocky gorge, the river benefits from the verticality of its host valley, and many mountain seeps and small tributaries actually cool the river down a bit.

Let's now look more closely at what the fisherman can expect on those sections of the Neversink open to the public.

One October, a friend and I planned a backpacking trip for deer. In studying my topo maps in preparation for this trip, it dawned on me that the Neversink's East Branch might be the only place where one could truly backpack for trout in the Catskills. To be more specific, no other Catskill river met all these requirements: (1) was two hours' or more hiking time from any road; (2) was open to the public for fishing; and (3) was a stream of reason-

*The accessible water on the Neversink above the reservoir
is small water, but the brookies are there. Good water flows plus favorable
stream temperatures equal success.*

able size and one that would be permanent (always have water). On that deer hunting trip, the river was wide and beautiful looking even two hours upstream from the Denning trailhead parking lot. Since in October Catskill streams are typically quite low, I assumed that the river must always have enough water to hold brook trout. In checking with the conservation department, I confirmed my fears that there might be an acid rain problem in these clear, high, infertile headwaters. While pH readings as low as 4.1 had in fact been observed in the East Branch, biologists still found some trout. How far up those trout existed, and whether the acidity had worsened, were the two remaining questions.

When we finally backpacked in for trout it was May, and we were shocked at how low the river was for midspring. It was discouraging, but it didn't stop us. We fished for two days and caught many brookies, some of which we cooked up at our base camp near the lean-to. On that particular trip, I caught or observed trout (strictly brookies) as far up as Donovan Brook. But even upstream of Donovan, there were pools and holes certainly deep enough to hold a 10-inch-or-better brookie. The trout we caught were mostly 5 to 7 inches, with a few smaller ones and a few up to about 9 inches. The water on May 20 was a nippy 55 degrees. The only fly life we observed was a small, yellowish stonefly that appeared every day. The trout were very unchoosy about what artificial flies they would take. The following year we went in again and curiously, while the water was colder, there was more variety to the fly life. Those same yellow stoneflies were present, but there were also some large mayflies that looked like quill Gordons. The water was in the high 40s, and the trout weren't biting at all.

As I've said, the East Branch below the Denning lean-to is all posted, and virtually all of the West Branch is private, so the next piece of public water is downstream of Neversink Reservoir. This is the meat 'n' potatoes of Neversink River trout fishing today.

The releases here are better than they once were, but they're still not what they should be. The minimum release from Neversink Reservoir from May 1 through September 30 is 53 cubic feet per second (cfs). This is much less than the June-through-August Pepacton minimum release of 95 cfs, and much, much less than the June-through-mid-September Cannonsville release of 160 cfs. In addition, New York City virtually never allows spillover from Neversink Reservoir. Rather, it will "draw like mad" from Neversink—according to one state official—not wanting to "waste" its high-quality water. Finally, the Neversink below the dam is tributary-poor, so even steady rains will only slowly swell the river. The end result of all this? Comparatively low water levels and trout fishing that isn't nearly what it would be if the cfs figure were doubled. It seems that no matter when you come here, you end up saying to yourself, "If only there were a little more water." In addition to this negative, human activity—mostly residential development—has increased exponentially between Hasbrouck and Route 17.

There is, though, more character to the river than you might think when you scan it from the road. Further, a few sections are somewhat secluded. Quite a number of wild trout exist from the dam down to Hasbrouck, and for this reason no stocking takes place. Trout are stocked from Hasbrouck down to South Fallsburg, and at a few points between South Fallsburg and Route 17.

The upper end in particular—because of its smallness—amplifies the problem anglers face on the entire river down to Route 17: low, clear, and fairly shallow water that makes approaching your quarry without spooking it most challenging. Careful wading and thoughtful presentation are essential here.

Mostly browns are present in the tailwater Neversink, but some nice brookies have been reported in that very cold water just below the dam for a mile or so. From that dam down to the first bridge, yellow signs inform you that there is no entrance for any purpose. But just below this bridge, white signs tell you the opposite, that fishing with a permit is okay. This means you need the watershed permit discussed on page 20. When I visited, there was some beaver work visible, as well as wild strawberry growing along the bank. I even spotted two northern water snakes at the edge of one of the large, dammed-up pools that characterize the beat down to Hasbrouck—but no brook trout came to net.

On the east bank not far below the first bridge below the dam is the large, privately owned Neversink River Campgrounds. Below this is an abandoned farm, its now fallow fields stretching widely to the river. Some access may be possible here. When you get down to the second bridge below the dam, right at Hasbrouck (see the map), state easements start to kick in. Cross the bridge from east to west, then turn left toward Woodbourne. After a short way you'll see the first DEC access sign and you will have to drive down an old washboard road to get to the river. You'll notice that there is a lot of flat water here and throughout the tailwater Neversink all the way down to the gorge.

The second DEC access sign is only a short way downstream or south of the first. Parking is right there, and the river practically touches the road. Local residents often fish bait in this very deep pool, with rods propped up on forked sticks. You have just enough headroom for false casting here, but what you really want to do is wade up and around to the left to get at the twin riffles, separated by an island, that head the pool. There are frequently trout rising in the riffles as well as in the pool, even in summer, and it's a good place to settle in for the evening hatch. Here, as at other points on the river, streambank trash is quite noticeable.

At the next bridge, where Route 42 crosses the river, the village of Woodbourne intrudes upon the river. Yet below this there are again some farm fields, active or abandoned, although parts of the river here are highly exposed to the sun. There are no easements here, and access is questionable.

As you continue south on Route 42, two more easily spotted DEC access signs are visible on your left, right around Fallsburg. Each has parking, and each gives you a short beat of river to fish. I've always liked the section behind the municipal garage (another bumpy road down to the parking spot and river), where I have fly-fished up some bright brownies from fairly nice, shady runs. The well-trod path that heads north from the parking lot through a grove of small hornbeams lets you know that you're not the only one who fishes these easement sections.

I don't know what to tell you about that section near South Fallsburg. This garish, Coney Island–like community does not remind one of frontier America. The human commotion spills over from the streets and theaters down to the riverbank. Nonetheless, there are a few short easements right in town.

Below South Fallsburg there are a few intriguing sections of the river, and if you have a local road map or a topo you'll find some water to your liking between South Fallsburg and the Quickway bridge. There are several very substantial easements here. A long one stretches north from Avon Lodge Road on the west bank. Another pushes north from Route 17, also on the west bank (easements can be to just one side of the river or to both). You shouldn't find many other anglers on these two. Although there are no public easements, you might want to navigate local roads and see if you can find some open water between the Quickway bridge and the gorge, a beat that Ray Bergman mentioned in his classic book *Trout* in a little discussion of the "Bridgeville Olives."

The celebrated Neversink Gorge was formerly owned by the Orange & Rockland Power Company, and was off limits to the general public. In 1981 the state purchased the lands bordering the gorge, and created the Neversink Gorge State Unique Area. It later purchased the fishing and hunting rights, which were owned by an individual. The state did not rest on these accomplishments but continued to buy adjacent land, and with the recent acquisition of 1,600 acres the unique area now stands at about 7,000 acres.

These 6.5 miles of gorgeous, shady river, scarcely more than an hour and a half from New York City, are completely undeveloped and truly wild looking, and since a substantial hike is required to get down to the water, the angling pressure is light. Two friends and I visited the gorge this past May. In a whole day of fishing (it was a weekday) we saw only one other angler, far in the distance. The mayflies were hatching as they were supposed to be, the caddisflies were buzzing about, and when long shadows erased the bright glare on the water's surface, sharp-looking browns up to 14 inches and wild brookies up to an honest foot started to belt my dry fly. We found little in the way of established paths along the river, and in fact the bank is so steep in spots that you have to be a billy goat just to make your way up- or downstream. May it remain this way, for it will help to keep this place special.

While a few stocked browns may drift down from upriver sections that are stocked, most gorge fish are thought to be wild. The brookies are apparently not uncommon.

The water character here couldn't be any nicer. Deep sheltering pools alternate with long riffles, and there are wonderful escarpment pools, countless boulders, shelflike rapids, and other features that bring to mind a wild Adirondack river. However, this was just one trip, and water levels were ideal. The fish are there, but the fishability during lower water would have to be tested over several other trips.

All this mileage within the gorge has been designated no-kill, the season runs from April 1 through October 15, and only artificial lures may be used. Parking is very limited, and while the most popular parking spots for those using the gorge are depicted on the map on page 60, you'll definitely want to bring a good road map when exploring this area. Right now the gorge is for day use only. Overnight camping is not allowed.

Immediately below the gorge roads are nearly absent, and although this is private water, one official described the posting as "intermittent." From the spot where the stream flows under Route 49 down to the Basher Kill the stream may become increasingly warm, but there are still trout. DEC stocks trout in the vicinity of Route 209 and wild trout have been seen even downstream of this. In addition, the tenacious efforts of DEC personnel have paid off in the form of several more public easements to this off-the-beaten-path water downstream of Oakland.

At present there is parking and some open water—beautiful water indeed—at the Route 49 bridge. From this point down to Route 209 there are some houses and a lot of posting, but there is one point at which the stream comes very close to the road, and here there is an easement and parking right next to the stream. This is wide, rocky, fast water that brings to mind parts of the Beaver Kill. I suspect that it's very lightly fished.

There is another easement a way below this, and you can also park at the north corner of the steel bridge that spans the Neversink at Route 209 and fish downstream. Finally, there is an easement just above the confluence with the Basher Kill. Warm-water species like bass and panfish almost totally displace trout in the final stretch of the Neversink from the Basher Kill down to the Neversink's confluence with the main stem of the Delaware at Port Jervis. But there's another finfish worth targeting here: Shad enter the Neversink in spring and can make it upstream to 1 mile above Route 209, where a dam stops their progress. One popular spot for shad fishing is by the D&H Canal Museum at Cuddebackville.

Schoharie Creek

Schoharie Creek is the shy schoolgirl who stands alone in a corner on Saturday night, and I am among the guilty who have failed to ask her to dance. Although I did fish this stream many years ago, mostly when I headed to this part of the Catskills it was to hunt snowshoe rabbits in the Jewett Range. Yet I felt obligated to learn a little more about this important Catskill river, and that kind of obligation is what makes a project of this nature worthwhile.

The Schoharie rises about 6 miles northwest of the village of Saugerties and flows roughly northwest for some 21 miles as the crow flies before meeting Schoharie Reservoir near Prattsville. There are many more miles of the Schoharie below the reservoir, and this less-than-spectacular warm-water fishing is briefly discussed in chapter 8.

Traversing a very steep part of the Catskills, the upper Schoharie, that section discussed in this chapter, nevertheless rides through a fairly broad valley, and its flows are very much enhanced by the contributions of three smaller but significant streams: the East Kill, the West Kill, and the Batavia Kill (see chapter 7). The river is dominated by Route 23, the reconstruction of which in the 1960s proved detrimental to the Schoharie. There is also a large and growing negative impact from human activity in the valley (especially near the large ski resort at Hunter), much of it related to tapping of the watershed for drinking purposes. Perhaps the broadest problem is the one that has most affected other Catskill rivers: the removal of hemlocks and other native trees that once grew thick to the bank, keeping water temperatures down and water levels more stable. Another handicap is the width of the channel—that is, the distance between the banks that define the usual high-water mark. Because of the frequent flooding and the high precipitation in this area, the channel has been expanded so that most of the time it's considerably wider than the actual width of the flowing water. This further opens up the river to the effects of the sun. Sharp flow fluctuations and summer temperatures that frequently run into the mid-80s depress Schoharie Creek trout fishing.

Although the state has tried special regulations, today only general statewide angling regulations are in effect: five trout daily, no size limit. Surveys show that fishing pressure here may actually be lighter than it was a few decades ago, possibly due in part to competition from the now very productive Catskill tailwaters.

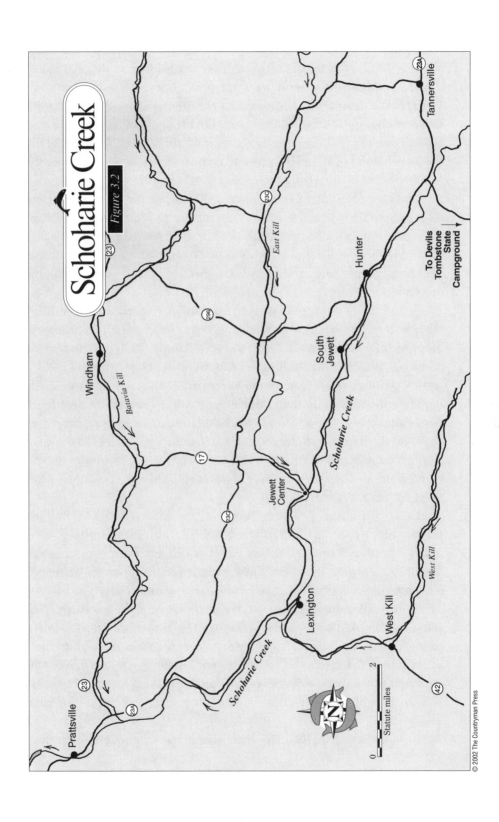

Schoharie Creek

Figure 3.2

Prattsville

Windham

Batavia Kill

Schoharie Creek

Lexington

Jewett Center

Schoharie Creek

West Kill

West Kill

South Jewett

Hunter

East Kill

Tannersville

To Devils
Tombstone
State
Campground

N

0   2
Statute miles

Upstream or southeast of Hunter there are about 6 stream miles of interesting small water to work. It's rocky and shaded here, with nice holding lies, reasonably stable water flows, and reportedly abundant insect hatches. With tall mountains for a backdrop and exquisitely water-sculpted bedrock in places, this upper Schoharie water is redoubtable. Look at your road map and run your finger along the most convenient road between Tannersville and the artsy hamlet of Elka Park. At one point you'll cross a bridge over the Schoharie, and as of recently, there was access here.

The approximately 18 stream miles of the Schoharie below Hunter are more open to the sun, and flows can fluctuate dramatically. Geography actually plays a dirty trick on the river. Since it tracks essentially east to west, it's exposed to the sun all day long. Streams that run on a more north–south axis don't have this problem. And, as I've said, that wide channel compounds the problem.

From Hunter down to Lexington trout still dominate, and this is likely the most popular stretch of the Schoharie. Below Lexington, the smallmouth bass which are actually seen all the way up to Hunter really start to become numerous, while the trout fishing worsens as you head downstream from this small Catskill hamlet. Here in the lower part of the river, the steep, surrounding mountains do their double dirty work: They send down fierce floods after a heavy rain to erode the Schoharie, then—tapped out—they choke off the river until flows become paltry and warm. Still, I did some exploring on the Schoharie this summer, and even with the low, warm water, I found good numbers of nice-sized trout in isolated deep pools just a few miles upstream of Prattsville.

Despite its several significant problems, the Schoharie also has its good points. Fishing pressure is comparatively light. As with any river that you initially judge from the road, there are plenty of delightful surprises when you actually get down to the water. These include deep holding lies where you probably didn't expect them. The Schoharie also affords very good access. There are 6 miles of state easements, essentially between the low barrier dam and Cook Brook. There are also about five Department of Transportation parking lots along Route 23, and for the most part the water next to these lots is unposted. On this subject, you cannot assume that where a river runs right next to the road—whether or not there's a parking lot—the banks are necessarily public property. But if they aren't posted, you can, in this state, legally fish.

In addition to the DOT lots, there are numerous other pull-offs where anglers may park along Route 23 without being questioned. There are also some back roads by which to explore the river. Hamlets are far apart in the valley, and the second-home devlopment that is taking place here is mainly near the ski resort at Hunter.

A sage piece of advice offered by Schoharie Creek veterans is to hit the stream early in the season before the dual problems of low flows and high temperatures occur. From June 1 onward, most Schoharie devotees recommend that you try at dawn or from dusk through darkness. Another good piece of advice is to read the late Art Flick's *New Streamside Guide to Naturals and Their Imitations.* Flick, the legendary Catskill fly-fisherman and conservationist who died in 1986, made his home in West Kill for many years and did much of his research for the book on the Schoharie. An expert angler, he was considered the unchallenged master of this stream, and his legacy here lives on.

In the headwaters upstream of Hunter, wild brook trout predominate, though there are also some wild browns and wild rainbows; this section is not stocked. Below Hunter, DEC surveys show that mostly stocked browns are present, with a few rainbows seen now and again. A whopping 95 percent of the browns caught are stocked fish, and that wild-trout figure of only 5 percent is the worst of any major Catskill river. Further, among the stocked fish only about 15 percent will be holdovers at any given time. Each year the DEC stocks the Schoharie with about 15,000 trout, strictly browns.

Unusual Fish of the Region

One lazy day in late June I was wandering along the upper West Branch of the Delaware River. Its flows greatly diminished by weeks of rainless skies, the river was laying bare all its secrets; only the bottoms of the deepest pools were still hiding.

Just below an unenthusiastic riffle I spotted a strange-looking fish. It was about 18 to 19 inches long and very portly in its anterior section. The caudal peduncle seemed quite long, and the tail was small. Overall it was a brownish amber color, and it had light-colored, wavy bars along its flank. What was it? Discussions with various experts led to no conclusion, nor did a dimly lit journey through several guidebooks back at the hunting camp that night.

What strange, watery denizens occur in Catskill and nearby waters? Refugees or transplants from the home aquarium are always a possibility, but there are a number of natural oddballs, too.

The bowfin is one of the most curious and also one of the most primitive. Scientifically it is *Amia calva,* and it has such occult common names as dogfish, grindle, grinnel, and cypress trout. The bowfin is the lone survivor of a family of ancient fish, as determined by fossil remains in Europe and the United States. This relic can reach a length of up to 3 feet and a weight of up to 20 pounds.

The bowfin seems to prefer shallow, weedy lakes and slow-moving streams, but that's not a hard-and-fast rule. According to range maps it's more common in the Southeast, but it does extend up to our area and beyond to the St. Lawrence drainage. In our region, the bowfin not only is found in the Basher Kill marsh but is also common enough there that it's cursed by the great marsh's bass devotees. The bowfin has also turned up in the watershed reservoirs from time to time—for example, West Branch Reservoir—and is known to exist in the main stem of the Delaware; recently a specimen was even captured in the Delaware's East Branch. Most bowfin are taken incidentally in our area by anglers trying for other fish. Surprised fishermen find that this often weighty creature puts up a dogged fight. Some anglers have put their finger into the mouth of a bowfin, and wished they hadn't.

Although bowfin are surely not pulchritudinous, the sea lamprey *(Petromyzon marinus)* has to get the ugly award among Catskill fish. This primitive, eel-shaped creature is a parasitic, anadromous fish that, like the shad, ascends the Delaware River to spawn each spring. They are common not only in the main Delaware, but also up into the East Branch and even the Beaver Kill. I personally have observed them as far upstream as Wagon Tracks Pool on the Beaver Kill, and last season I apparently bore witness to three lampreys—presumably two males and one female—spawning in a thin riffle on the Delaware's East Branch. Lampreys are also found in the Hudson and tributaries to the Hudson. Before the Philipsburg Manor dam in Sleepy Hollow was restored, they used to run up my boyhood brook—the Pocantico River—in good numbers. They are also known to occur in Rondout Creek up to about Rosendale. I've long heard that baby lampreys can be dug up in certain river sandbars in the Delaware, and that they make good bait for walleyes and smallmouths. I'm informed that they can be legally used only along the border-water portions of the West Branch and the main stem. In any case, as near as I can tell this Delaware River folk bait is drifting into obscurity.

The channel catfish, *Ictalurus punctatus,* also turns up in the Catskill region. They are very rare here, and where they do occur have probably been privately stocked. A whopping 20^1/$_2$-pounder was wrested from Sullivan County's White Lake in the early 1980s; they have a picture of this fearsome-looking cat at the New Paltz office of the DEC. Channel cats have also been observed in the "Sturgeon Pool," a widening of the Wallkill River just before it joins Rondout Creek in Ulster County.

The cisco *(Coregonus artedii)* is yet another fish that is rare but present in this area. It's rare and maybe even disappearing in Ashokan Reservoir where in the past it averaged about 2 to 3 pounds. In Dutchess County's Sylvan Lake the cisco does occur, and a specimen also turned up recently in Kensico Reservoir. The cisco is sometimes called "lake herring" since it superficially resembles a herring, but it's really a part of the trout family, Salmonidae. It can be taken by a wide array of angling tricks, including ice fishing. A. J. McClane, in his *New Standard Fishing Encyclopedia,* claims that ciscoes rise to the surface for insects and can be taken on dry flies.

One more oddball: the gizzard shad, *Dorosoma cepedianum.* Formerly, it was extremely rare in the Catskill region, although it has long been documented in the Basher Kill marsh. But since about 1995, large numbers of gizzard shad have been ascending the Delaware River system, and have been distributing themselves even into tributaries of the Willowemoc. In at least two of the past five years, they have been abundant in the drainage as far upriver as Parksville.

Gizzard shad seem to be expanding their range, and have become so numerous in some watersheds that biologists are concerned about their possible impact on more desirable species. I've found—and caught—them in great numbers in tributaries to the lower Hudson River in recent years, but I've never taken one home. They're said to be just awful on the table.

CHAPTER 4

The Beaver Kill
and Willowemoc

Fly-fishing is a sport of romance, and in all its lexicon of tradition and romance there is no more sacred a name than this: Beaver Kill! Quite possibly the best-known trout stream in the world, this 42-mile river flows through a land that is itself steeped in romance. It is the Catskill Mountains, a place whose strange, somber beauty has been sought but never quite captured by two centuries of writers and artists.

Several times man has placed the Beaver Kill on the gallows; each time it has refused to die. Deforestation from logging was an early ill. The hide-tanning industry of the 19th century, which used hemlock bark as its raw material, helped denude the watershed, and spewed its noxious wastes into the river. On the heels of that enterprise came the "acid factories," which relied on hardwood trees and which also spewed toxic substances into the helpless Beaver Kill. This river industry took a toehold in the late 19th century, but the last factory in the mountains—at what is now the famous Acid Factory Pool in Horton—didn't close its doors until the early 1950s. But even as this mountain industry was dying, engineers with the New York State Department of Transportation were drafting some new mischief. It was the new Route 17, the so-called Quickway, which was built in the 1960s. That bitterly fought road—which crossed the Beaver Kill and Willowemoc Rivers 13

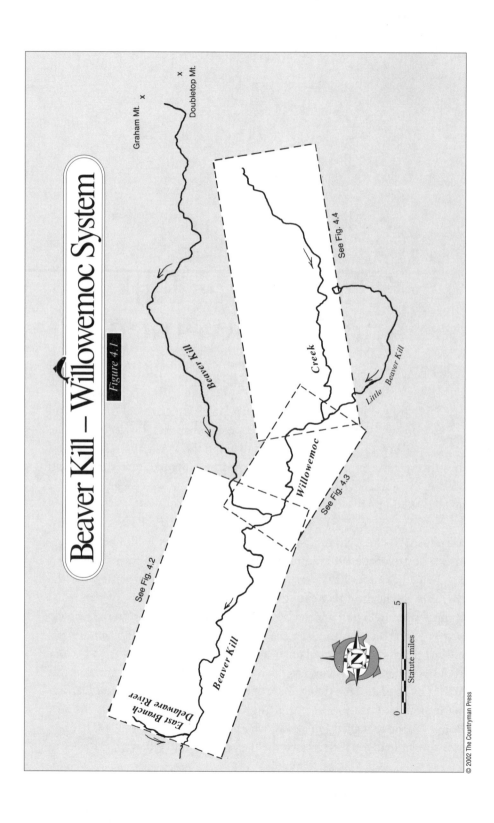

Beaver Kill – Willowemoc System

Figure 4.1

Graham Mt. x

Doubletop Mt. x

Beaver Kill

See Fig. 4.4

Creek

Little Beaver Kill

Willowemoc

See Fig. 4.3

See Fig. 4.2

Beaver Kill

East Branch Delaware River

Statute miles

0   5

© 2002 The Countryman Press

times—is now omnipresent on what is usually called the "Big Beaver Kill" below Roscoe. Yet many of the temporary wounds of the road building have healed, and with the enactment of special regulations and the rise of new angler philosophies, the Beaver Kill once again offers excellent trout fishing by the standards of many.

The Willowemoc is the Beaver Kill's sister stream. The two are often discussed together, and so it is in this chapter. Yet the Willow is a smaller stream, and there are other differences, too.

This equally classic stream rises in the mountains of Ulster County south of the upper Beaver Kill. It flows south and west to join the Beaver Kill at the celebrated Junction Pool at Roscoe. As I discuss each river, starting with the Beaver Kill, study the maps—figures 4.1 through 4.4. First I'll go over the important subject of access.

Above or upstream of Junction Pool it's sometimes called the Little Beaver Kill, while below Junction Pool it's occasionally called the Big Beaver Kill. This nomenclature is hazardous, though, because not only is there a Little Beaver Kill that feeds the Willowemoc (see chapter 7), but there's also both a Beaver Kill and Little Beaver Kill that feed the Esopus in a different part of the Catskills. Here I'll use the terms upper Beaver Kill and lower Beaver Kill when referring to the two sections of this river.

Regrettably, the upper Beaver Kill is virtually all private water. At the extreme headwaters, east of the trailhead to Round Pond, the uppermost 2 miles or so do bisect state land. There may be very small brook trout here, though I've not tried it.

Below the Round Pond trailhead, one private angling club after another has locked up gorgeous stretches of the river, and I couldn't find any public access to this upper mileage. You will have to be very well connected to have a hope of gaining membership to any of these clubs.

Actually, you do have at least one means of baptizing your waders in this hallowed upper Beaver Kill water, but you will have to pay for it. You can stay at the Beaverkill Valley Inn near Lew Beach, and fish the inn's private mile of river (fly-fishing only). Beautifully restored by Larry Rockefeller, nephew of the late New York State governor Nelson A. Rockefeller, the inn has a little bar and stone fireplaces, and it serves home-cooked meals. Rates range from $135 to $205 per person per night based on double occupancy (plus sales tax and gratuity), but that includes three meals, tennis, pool, trail use, and of course, fishing. Call for reservations.

Heading downstream, the nonaffiliated angler gets his first crack at the

Beaver Kill at the state-run Beaver Kill Campground (also called the Covered Bridge Campground), where there is an old covered bridge. There are approximately 2 miles of public water here, and of course if you like to camp the possibilities will be obvious to you. The facility is open from April 1 through Labor Day, and rates are very reasonable. Scenic and quiet, this is also a superb place to stop for a restful lunch, with picnic tables and grills available. If it's a hot day, you can even take a dip in the big pool by the bridge, an activity that seems to no longer be actually sanctioned here.

Although brookies are still present, by this point the water is of a fair size and scrappy browns also fin the currents. As you might imagine, this short section gets hit quite hard, but in early spring in particular there are plenty of fish to go around.

The next piece of public water is from the bridge at Cat Hollow Road (Route 206) just above Rockland downstream to Roscoe. On this 2-mile-plus stretch the state has secured permanent easements for fishing. The river here is still fairly small, about perfect for a 5-weight fly-rod system. The trout are mostly browns, and they are sleek and sophisticated. Specifically, access to the stream can be gained via several dirt roads or pull-offs from Route 206 that lead down to the water. A state parking lot for anglers is located just off Route 206 in the hamlet of Rockland and is well marked.

There are guaranteed easements to almost the entire lower Beaver Kill, from Junction Pool downstream to the river's confluence with the East Branch of the Delaware River at the hamlet of East Branch. To understand these easements, see the essay in chapter 7. All you need do is drive along old Route 17 from Roscoe downstream, and where to park will be obvious.

There are two no-kill areas on the Beaver Kill. The first is from the Sullivan County line a short way below Roscoe downstream for 2.5 miles, the second from 1 mile upstream to 1.6 miles downstream of the Iron Bridge at Horton. On both, fishing is permitted year-round, but only artificial lures may be used and all trout must be immediately returned. Streambank signs delineate the extent of these special-regulation sections.

These rules have dramatically increased the average size and number of trout present. Of the 25,000 trout (mostly browns) that are annually stocked in the Beaver Kill, a good many now make it to 14 inches or better; 14- to 18-inch fish are relatively common, while 19- to 22-inch fish are very much present. One day a friend measured a 24-inch brown trout that had washed up dead at Wagon Tracks Pool. Even bigger ones are probably present.

The distinct majority of fish taken in the Beaver Kill are from stockings.

*Hendrickson's Pool, one of the most famous on the Beaver Kill.
It lies within the upper no-kill stretch.*

Only some 10 percent are wild fish. This percentage is increasing, however, because rainbows are slowly infiltrating the river from a downstream direction. It should be noted, too, that there are many holdover browns in the Beaver Kill, and after a season or two in the stream these stocked fish do take on the firmness and coloration of their wild kin.

The no-kill sections with their oversized brownies are understandably busy, and getting busier. These days, the no-kills are even crowded on weekdays, though somewhat less so Tuesday through Thursday. There are also fewer anglers from August through October than in the first four months of the season.

Between the no-kill sections there is some interesting water, and this piece is cast to by both fly- and spin-fishermen. Then there is that former haunt of mine, the lower end of the lower Beaver Kill. Only a decade ago you could escape to here. Now even this beat gets a lot of pressure, especially where the road runs close by.

This lower part of the river carves an increasingly deep valley, and it runs wider and in some places deeper. Although it also runs warmer—more chubs—the trout seem to have little problem riding out the doldrums near tributaries or more commonly just cold "seeps" coming off the mountains. I have often wondered if the trout may possibly migrate upstream to escape summer temperatures.

Most people who fish the Bea-Moc find the services they need between Roscoe and Livingston Manor. There are well-stocked shops in both communities, as well as in the little hamlet of Deckertown in between. There are also many hotels, motels, and campgrounds in this area, as well as restaurants plain and fancy. Roscoe is more the hub of angling activity than is Livingston Manor, but it should be said that this entire area of the Catskills caters to visitors, and accommodations of all types exist. For some interesting and fact-filled brochures along these lines, contact the Roscoe Chamber of Commerce, Roscoe, NY 12776.

There is pleasantly more public water on the upper Willowemoc than on the upper Beaver Kill. Again, I'll start at the headwaters and work downstream.

This stream, too, can be divided into two sections. From its source to Livingston Manor, the Willow is a small to medium-sized stream, and along this stretch there are several pieces of public water. In its headwaters, the stream branches off just above the little hamlet of Willowemoc. One branch is called Fir Brook, and although I haven't fished it recently, when I did it was alive with little brookies averaging 5 to 7 inches. There is increasing camp development near Fir Brook, but happily there is also considerable state land. First off, there is a lengthy easement just above the junction with the Willowemoc's main branch. In spring, flows are healthy here, but from late spring through fall this easement water gets very thin. Carefully seek out the deeper holes and you should be rewarded with those pan-sized, brightly colored natives. As you move upstream, Fir Brook is off the road and weaves in and out of forest preserve land. It's actually deeper and slower here, thanks to the work of the local beaver population. Even as you read this beavers are gnawing and cutting, dragging and placing, intent on their master plan of turning this entire upper drainage into Lake Willowemoc. Explorers take note: The swampy conditions here keep most anglers away.

The main branch of the Willowemoc above the hamlet of that name contains more water, and here too there is a fine population of wild brookies. Some of these will go an honest 10 or 11 inches, and there are some other surprises. One day after a May shower, I was working a salted minnow and taking many nice speckled trout. At a deep logjam, I let the minnow work with the current and down into the foam that marked the fringe of the

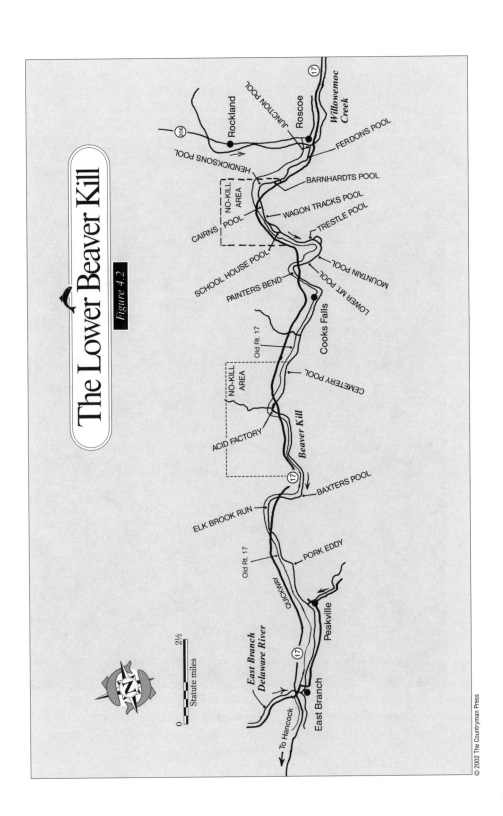

The Lower Beaver Kill

Figure 4.2

Statute miles

© 2002 The Countryman Press

A glimpse of one of the productive runs on the lower part of the lower Beaver Kill. Although the water does run warmer here and there are more chubs, both browns and rainbows are in ample supply. Certain pools hold 3- and 4-pound trout.

tangle. A jarring strike snapped me out of my upstream torpor, and I soon coaxed a marvelously colored, 14-inch brown out of the jam. I reasoned that it might well have been a wild fish, but in any case, it sure made those little brookies in my wicker creel look pitiful.

Above the junction with Fir Brook, the main branch of the Willowemoc and its several little feeders wend their way quite far into the mountains. There is beaver work here, too, creating holding water where there had been none before. You have to drive quite far upstream to reach the point above which it is all forest preserve, but for brook trout fanciers it's worth it, since the extreme upper Willow carves some pleasantly deep holding water.

Both above and below Butternut Brook is private water, and posted. Just above the junction with Fir Brook, however, the Willowemoc bisects the forest preserve, and while this short public section was turned inside out by the January flood of 1996, it's starting to normalize, and there are some nice pools. Park judiciously due to often swampy conditions.

Just below this piece of forest preserve water is the privately run Willowemoc Campground, but just below this is a state easement, marked by a sign, that opens up a pleasant section of river. I've always been able to count on a few richly colored brookies from this section, and on my last trip I was surprised at how many browns mixed into the catch. Beavers are at work here, too, changing the shape of the water.

There is more good news below this. From just below the hamlet of Willowemoc and downstream several miles, the state has secured easements for fishermen. In the middle of this stretch is the Willowemoc Covered Bridge Campground, privately owned and very popular with camping anglers. By this point the river has gained steam, and now there is much better room and opportunity for fly-casting.

Just above and below Mongaup Creek—a very nice stream for small trout—the Willow is mostly private. Then state easements begin again, stretching a number of miles on and off down to the Quickway bridge. On this bigger water, browns of over 18 inches are caught every year. Nonetheless, I have to concur with other Catskill writers who have spoken of less-than-auspicious angling on this part of the 'Moc.

From Livingston Manor down to Roscoe—the "Big Willowemoc," you might say—the water is almost all public via state easements. If the lower Beaver Kill or the Delaware is a little big for you, this stretch of the Willow might just fit your style. It's beautiful, classic fly-fishing water, and the entire river can be covered from one side. Hatches are very good, and the water is diverse. Further, there is a protective no-kill section, which extends from 1,200 feet above the mouth of Elm Hollow Brook downstream 3.5 miles to the second Quickway bridge east of Roscoe. Some of my most memorable Catskill fishing has been on this part of the Willowemoc, especially just above and below the rest area on Route 17 (you can park there).

One drizzly, early-May day when I was very new to fly-fishing, I hit a hatch of quill Gordons near the rest area. I took a dozen fish, the largest around 18 inches, and that textbook encounter—1:30 P.M. sharp—cemented my attraction to the long rod. I have subsequently had great fun fishing a May caddis in the picturesque water above the rest area. I also very much like the section from Roscoe up to the first bridge. Because it's so shady, this stretch will fish better on a hot day, and the lack of parking keeps pressure relatively light. I've always parked along the Quickway to fish this section, but with that road soon to become an interstate, you may have to make other plans. You can double your pleasure here in early season by running into both Hendricksons and little blue quills.

With the advent of no-kill and year-round trout fishing, anglers have discovered that Beaver Kill and Willowemoc trout can be taken in the off-months. Catskill winters are normally rough, so the earliest you'll usually see anyone astream is March. From the middle of that month through most of April, comparatively few trout will be seen rising to naturals on the surface. Sport shops and saloons in the area are fond of scribbling "what's hatching" on their blackboards, and in early season you'll usually see EARLY BROWN or EARLY BLACK STONEFLIES posted. You may see a few of these, you may see a few small blue-winged olives, often size 16 and smaller, and you will probably see a few caddis. But with normal weather, you will seldom see a good rise of fish before April 20. Better to probe the depths with nymphs or various simulative sinking patterns.

Though I have encountered relatively few quill Gordon hatches, and those mostly years ago, when I have it's been between April 29 and May 7. The first week of May may also see the appearance of little blue quills (*Paraleptophlebia* species) and/or two *Baetis* species. I've found that this can be one of the best hatches on the Bea-Moc, and one that can elicit a very active rise of fish. The little size 16 and 18 sailboat duns seem to have difficulty rising in the cold water, and the trout sip away steadily and methodically. A well-tied hackle-tip olive is deadly for the *Paraleptophlebia* hatch.

The Hendrickson *(Ephemerella subvaria)* seems to be a durable hatch that holds up well on rivers where other, perhaps more sensitive mayflies have disappeared. The first week of May can be prime time on the Bea-Moc, but with the warm weather we've been having, good *E. subvaria* hatches have appeared in mid- to late April. In any case, this is a hatch that fly-casters miss on many rivers because they go too late. The large, size 12 Hendricksons normally evoke a very good rise of fish on both the Beaver Kill and the Delaware. Nonetheless, in each of the last five years I've made a one-day trip to the Beaver Kill–Delaware watershed to fish the Hendricksons, and in three of those five years there were either no bugs or no trout rising to the bugs. There are no guarantees, especially in early season, but when it does come together this is one of the best times for the fly-fisher on the Beaver Kill–Delaware watershed. The hatching is dependable. Trout rise eagerly, and big trout are among them. Fishing pressure is somewhat less than in midseason. Confusing complex hatches are uncommon. Hatching periods can sometimes be very long—all afternoon and, occasionally, into the evening. Brush has not yet grown up along the riverbanks—a big factor on the main stem of the Delaware, where lush growth later in the season makes foot access to many sections difficult. Daytime temperatures are usually pleasantly cool, although nasty weather and roily water are certainly possible at this time.

About the same time these early-season mayflies are on the water, the celebrated "shadfly"—also called "grannom" but scientifically *Brachycentrus numerosus*—appears. This often blizzardlike hatch of caddisflies is something to witness. One year I brought my girlfriend up to the Beaver Kill to show her how to fly-fish. Well, the grannoms were so thick that they were getting in her ears and hair, and they actually scared her off the river. Fly-fishing canceled on account of too many bugs! Nonetheless, I've seldom seen this spectacular hatch prompt much of a surface rise, if any. The experts say, "Try pupal imitations," although this has rarely worked for me. Ed Van Put reports having some success using wet flies during the grannom hatch.

The period from about May 7 to May 24 can be a strange time on the Beaver Kill. The more or less predictable early-season hatches have largely passed, and the reasonably dependable midseason hatches haven't quite begun. If low pressure prevails, it will be wet, windy, and often surprisingly chilly. One year on May 24 a friend and I arrived to float the East Branch Delaware and heard of frost and snow flurries the night before. On the other hand, it can also be blazing hot if sunny skies predominate. If it's somewhere

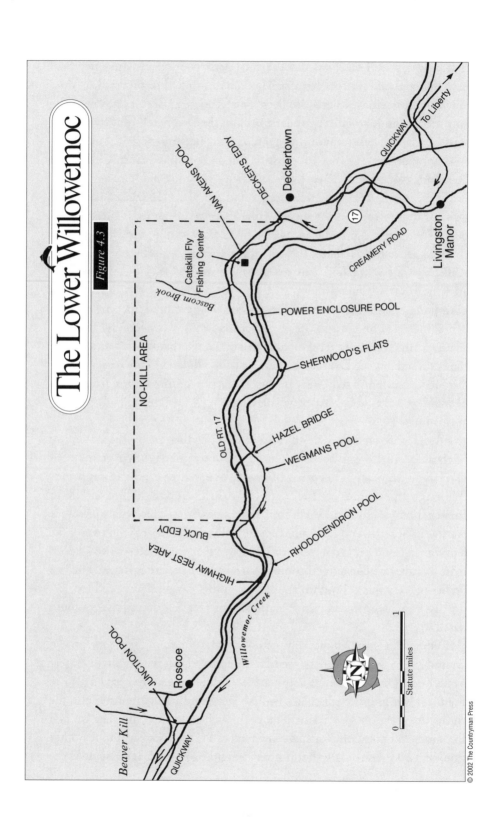

The Lower Willowemoc

Figure 4.3

VAN AKENS POOL

DECKER'S EDDY

Deckertown

Catskill Fly
Fishing Center

Bascom Brook

POWER ENCLOSURE POOL

SHERWOOD'S FLATS

NO-KILL AREA

OLD RT. 17

HAZEL BRIDGE

WEGMANS POOL

BUCK EDDY

RHODODENDRON POOL

HIGHWAY REST AREA

Willowemoc Creek

JUNCTION POOL

Roscoe

Beaver Kill

QUICKWAY

QUICKWAY

To Liberty

CREAMERY ROAD

Livingston Manor

17

Statute miles

0   1

in between, with moderate temperatures, average rain, and lots of cloudy, drizzly, misty days, you might encounter some excellent fly-fishing.

May 15 is smack in the middle of this sometimes dead period, and the date was running true to form when I got to the Peakville pool a number of years ago. No trout were rising, but there was a smattering of small, light caddis in the air. Still well back from the bank I studied the scene, then knotted on a size 16 elk hair caddis.

The river was at a normal height, and the little subpool where Trout Brook enters looked seductive but could not have been more than 6 inches deep. Still, that was where a little voice told me to cast. When I dropped the fly at the convergence point, there was a great cyclonic swirl, and the fish tore viciously out into the heart of the pool. I measured the 20-inch rainbow against some markings on my rod butt and thought about how even here in the timeless Catskills, things were changing.

Through May, you will often see some of those "other Hendricksons," *Ephemerella rotunda* and *E. invaria*—plus small blue-winged olives and various caddis. *E. rotunda* appears earlier in the season, while *E. invaria* can persist into early June and is definitely sometimes confused with *E. dorothea* (sulfur)—despite its being a hook size larger.

During May, March browns *(Stenonema vicarium)* may be present and to a lesser extent so may gray foxes *(S. fuscum),* though I've never seen either of these in great numbers. Don't let this fool you, though. Large mayflies hatching in small numbers can be a deadly happenstance, and with no fly is this more true than with the March brown. The lower end of the lower Beaver Kill often makes some March brown magic.

A dozen years ago, prominent outdoor writers who supposedly knew the Beaver Kill were penning articles affirming that this was strictly a brown trout stream. I was living in the mountains at the time, and I'd already known for several years that it was no longer so.

On June 3 in one of those years, I got to the Catskills for a two-day trip. I drove down to the lower Beaver Kill near Peakville at about 3:30 P.M., and when I got to the stream's edge I saw large stoneflies crawling all around the rocks. In the river there were only sporadic rises, but they were heavy ones. I knotted on a Humpy, a high-riding western fly that I'd used in the past during stonefly hatches. Its bouyancy lets you really twitch it in the riffles. After taking four good browns, I finally located what I was looking for: an eye-popping riseform in midstream. The fish took without hesitation, and 10 minutes later I slid a very beautiful 17-inch rainbow into the shallows. I'd taken a few rainbows in the lower river before, but this was the first big one.

The stonefly hatch waned, so I decided to drive down to the West Branch Delaware to see if any sulfurs had started yet. But the river was so high and roiled that I gave up and drove to Fish's Eddy on the East Branch. From the old steel bridge, rises were visible up and down as far as I could see standing on the bridge. It was a superb fall of coffin flies, but the fishing was very tough.

The next day at about 3 P.M. I headed on down to that same stretch of the lower Beaver Kill. All hell was breaking loose! The stoneflies were not to be seen, but there was a flotilla of *Isonychias* on the water, and other flies were present, too. Best of all, very large fish could be seen and heard splashing against the deep, far-stream channel. I worked over a brown of 3 to 4 pounds for a good 45 minutes but could not raise it. Now green drake duns were floating down the river, and there were also gray foxes and a few other flies I couldn't identify. I believe some of the big fish were taking emerging green drake nymphs—and they were extremely selective. Working upstream into the faster, more forgiving water, I watched a man above me land a rainbow of about 16 inches plus a smaller rainbow and a brown. All I could manage that afternoon, though, were two smallish browns. The big fish were just too tough for me.

Rainbows (all wild) are increasing in numbers in the Beaver Kill, and have had a significant presence in the lower river going back to at least 1990. Biologists have recently found rainbow fingerlings in small tributary streams far up into the Beaver Kill watershed, and the speculation is that this population will continue to expand. Almost certainly, this is a natural extension of the rainbow fishery in the Delaware River. As in the East Branch and the main stem, though, the rainbows seem to be largely but not totally oriented to the faster riffles. The browns in the lower Beaver Kill seem to be found in both the riffles and in the pools, with the bigger fish in the pools for sure.

To get back to Beaver Kill hatches in general, the celebrated green drake hatch is heavier on the lower Beaver Kill, and especially on the East Branch Delaware. This may be because there is more of the silty bottom that the burrowing green drake nymphs require. On the East Branch, the hatch may arrive as early as about May 23 or May 24, but on the lower Beaver Kill it will usually be five or six days later. I have found the trout to be extremely selective during this hatch, both to the duns and to the spinners. When the duns are especially numerous on the surface, the fishing can be exasperating as large, selective trout will be choosy in the extreme. When the duns are coming off sporadically, you can expect much better cooperation. Imitations for the spinner or "coffin fly" should be thoughtfully tied. I advise that you carry some fully spent and some fully hackled, because at times the spinners are really bouncing around and the full-hackled pattern works best. A good trick, if you're being frustrated during this hatch, is to move into slightly faster water where the trout cannot study your large imitation as well.

The first 10 days of June used to be a magical time on the Beaver Kill. Sadly, I've seen a sharp deterioration of insect life on the Beaver Kill over the past 30 years—my logbook goes back that far—and the once-impressive June hatches are not what they were. Development in the Beaver Kill Valley has gone on slowly but steadily, and now the Beaver Kill muddies up faster after a hard rain and clears up more slowly. Perhaps increased siltation has damaged the insect life that seemed so much richer when I started fishing this river.

And yet, from late May to late June, marvelous days can still occur.

One morning I arrived at Wagon Tracks Pool with some just-tied *Cornuta* floating nymphs, inspired by the fine book *Hatches*. When I got to the pool, several other anglers were working to a really good hatch but to little avail. Yet on my first cast I nailed a fat, 16-inch brown on my floating nymph. This is one of several nice, early-June hatches, but it can be a difficult one. Be prepared with a variety of patterns.

From about the second week of June well into July, you may also see other small blue-winged olives in the morning, the most important of which is *Ephemerella attenuata* in sizes 16 and 18. June is also a time of much caddis activity. At this time, when the water temperature is around 60 degrees and trout are very active, a vigorously worked caddis pupa can be deadly, even if relatively few flies are present on the surface. Early on a June morning you may also see some hatching stoneflies.

Sometimes there is a mid- to late-afternoon lull, but other times the fishing can be excellent all day long. This is especially true on cloudy, misty, windless days. But whatever happens during the day, there is always a strong possibility of a good evening rise in June.

At about 5:30 to 6 P.M., a very dark, size 12 to 14 caddis *(Psilotreta labida)* may appear. I've had great luck fishing this hatch while working an Adams at the bubbly heads of pools. The fly should be bounced actively. In some years jumbo *Isonychia* duns will start floating by and you may also see a terrific fall of coffin flies. Fish will be very selective. Sometime around 7:30 or

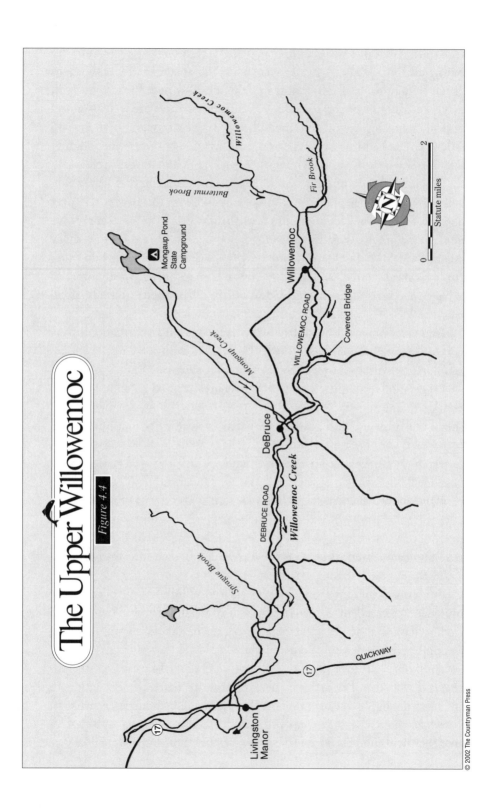

The Upper Willowemoc

Figure 4.4

Willowemoc Creek

Butternut Brook

Mongaup Pond State Campground

Fir Brook

Willowemoc

WILLOWEMOC ROAD

Covered Bridge

Mongaup Creek

DeBruce

DEBRUCE ROAD

Willowemoc Creek

Sprague Brook

QUICKWAY

17

Livingston Manor

17

N

0   2

Statute miles

8 P.M. sulfurs may appear, and my experience is that trout will almost always switch to them. Trout are ultrachoosy here. If a size 16 doesn't work, try an 18. There is often a fine line between the moment that trout are taking the sulfur duns and the moment they turn to spinners. Have both spent and semispent sulfur patterns, and observe carefully what's happening. Dick Talleur, in one of his articles about the Beaver Kill, says that trout will sometimes feed selectively to an emerger during the *E. dorothea* hatch.

To further complicate things during the June mix, there may be other flies, such as *Isonychia* spinners, on the water. One year I thrilled to the remarkable appearance of a *Hexagenia recurvata* hatch at Peakville. These enormous, strikingly colored mayflies flitted about like hummingbirds, and I didn't have anything in my vest even remotely large enough to imitate them. I thought about trying my hat for a moment but it was the wrong color. In any case, no trout were rising during this (for me) once-in-a-lifetime hatch. Maybe the trout were afraid of them.

From mid-June to early July, the morning activity gradually diminishes, and the duration of the evening hatch shrinks. The later in this period you go, the later the evening hatch. Yet I still like the period up to July 7 or so, when I can still have a hope of some kind of evening activity. For example, very light, large flies often lumped together under the heading "Cahills" can come off just before dark. Beyond that, there can be some on-and-off daytime activity to small blue-winged olives (possibly *E. attenuata* and two *Pseudocloeon* species), caddis, and a few other infrequent and lesser-known mayflies.

After about the first week of July and sometimes even sooner, the Beaver Kill becomes very low and, to me at least, unappealing. There is no question, though, that the serious fly-fisher can find delightful challenge and elbow room during the summer doldrums. Part of that challenge arrives in the form of the eye-straining "trico," a size 22 to 26 mayfly that hatches in the very early morning. This hatch can go on for weeks, from about early July to about mid-September, and although the insect is tiny, big fish can be drawn up. Tips for fishing this, the meat 'n' potatoes hatch of summer, can be found throughout the fly-fishing literature. If you're on the water between 5 and 8 A.M., you may be surprised by the appearance of other, unexpected mayflies. This is as true in late spring as it is in summer.

The primary hatching period for caddis is much longer than with mayflies. These sedges are something to watch for in high summer or in fact any time, since they help compensate for the mayfly hatches that have diminished.

Beaver Kill trout perk up dramatically in mid-September, and while mayfly hatching is minimal I do watch for Isonychias, which make a second and sometimes quite signicant reappearance in fall (actually, there are a few hatching all summer). When there are no mayflies, which is usual, trout—and trout fishermen—look to the landborne insects during this early-autumn period (if you don't know Catskill weather, autumn begins promptly on September 1).

Imitations of ants, hoppers, crickets, and so on can all be fished with success at certain times if you're stealthy enough to deal with the low water and you can find the right spot. Terrestrials may work best where heavy vegetation abuts or overhangs the river.

With the onset of autumn rains, and the continuing drop in water temperature, Beaver Kill trout can become extraordinarily active during the last week of September and the first two weeks of October. Fly-fishermen should experiment with ants, hoppers, beetles, and other terrestrial patterns, while still keeping an eye open for the odd late-season *Isonychia, Baetis,* or other aquatic insect. This is the time of year to forget the shackles of printed theory and stretch out with your own creativity.

In spring 2000 the New York State Department of Environmental Conservation, in cooperation with fisheries scientists from Cornell University, began a comprehensive study to determine the status and potential for enhancement of the trout resources of the Beaver Kill watershed. At the time of this writing, the study is ongoing, and it's not complete enough for me to cite scientific findings. But from it, one insight on angler use has come to light.

May and June saw the most fishing, with an estimated 20,116 and 20,201 angling hours spent on the watershed. No surprises there. April, July, and August registered 10,001, 9,895, and 8,783 hours, respectively. What caught my eye were the figures for autumn. Use dropped to just 5,667 hours in September, 3,243 hours in October, and 645 hours in November. More people fishing in August than in September and October? Draw your own conclusions.

By late October the water can become very cool, and action does start to taper. It depends on the weather. Many people fish the no-kill sections throughout November—surely with some success—but this is generally a cold month in the Catskills, although I remember a few shirtsleeve days. Whereas the no-kill stretches are open year-round, very little angler activity occurs on the Beaver Kill between December 1 and March 1, bank ice making it actually impossible much of that time.

Cooking Assertive-Tasting Fish

Some chefs use the degree of oiliness in a fish to determine a cooking method. For example, lean fish are often cooked by "fat" methods such as deep-frying or baking with butter, while fat fish are usually prepared by "dry" methods like barbecuing or broiling. There is merit to this, but I have a different approach. I choose the recipe based on how strong tasting I expect a fish to be or not to be. I don't just consider species, though; I also take into consideration what waters the fish have come from, and when. Freshwater fish in particular can vary tremendously in taste, with the prime example being trout. Despite their great mystique, no doubt born of the fact that some trout come from pure, cold, mountain streams, trout are quite far down on my list of favorite fish. True, I've had pink-fleshed wild brook trout from the Allagash River system that were delicious beyond compare, and fresh-caught lake trout from remote stillwaters in Ontario that could not be equaled by any supermarket fish. But I've also had muddy-tasting trout that needed a lot of embellishment to make them palatable. I've never had that problem with the plebeian yellow perch.

With my approach there are three categories of fish: mild, assertive tasting, and strong tasting. In the mild category I put flounder and most other flatfish, perch, whiting, hake and haddock, smelt, cod, certain salmon, and others. In the strong category I place bluefish, mackerel, tuna, and herring. I find, though, that the largest category is that of assertive-tasting fish, and many normally mild fish drift over into the strong category when taken from certain waters. Fish that are almost always assertive tasting—not necessarily in an unpleasant way—are striped bass, weakfish, most trout, crappies, sea bass, tom cod, black bass, and others.

Mild fish are best cooked simply, while strong fish can stand up to such ingredients as garlic, tomato sauce, anchovies, olives, peppers, and even red wine sauces. Assertive fish should be seasoned, but with a lighter hand. Handled just right, you can offset that slight "fishiness" and yet still allow the taste of the fish to come through.

Two of the most popular and widely used fish recipes are fish cakes and fish chowders. I developed my own through a long period of trial and error, tailoring them mostly to the assertive-tasting fish that I catch in southern New York and the Catskills. Two of the most popular fish in America will work well in these recipes: trout and black bass. Also try striped bass, bullheads, crappies, and other panfish you catch in this region.

No-Kill Fish Chowder

3 assertive-tasting fish, ¾ to 1 pound each, gutted and gilled

2 slices bacon, cut up

1 medium onion, diced

1 stalk celery with leaves, diced

1 medium carrot, peeled and diced

1 medium potato, peeled and diced

2 T. finely chopped parsley

Thyme leaves, ½ tsp. dried or ¼ tsp. powdered

Salt and white pepper to taste

3 c. milk

1 c. light cream

2 T. butter

3 T. flour

1. Scale the fish if possible. Cut each fish crosswise into four or five pieces. Put the pieces, including heads and tails, into a heavy nonreactive pot or Dutch oven and cover with 5 cups of water. Simmer gently for 30 minutes, stirring lightly two or three times.

2. Remove the fish with a slotted spoon and allow them to cool. Strain the broth through two layers of cheesecloth and reserve. When the fish pieces are cooled, remove all skin, fins, and bone and discard.

3. Clean the Dutch oven and in it, sauté the bacon pieces. Add the onion, celery, carrot, and potato and sauté until the carrot and potato have started to soften. Add the strained broth and bring to a simmer.

4. Add the fish meat, parsley, thyme, and salt and pepper and simmer gently for 30 minutes; stir once or twice but try to leave the fish chunks somewhat whole. Add the milk and cream and return to just below a boil. Taste for salt and add if necessary.

5. In the meantime, in a small pot or skillet, melt the butter and stir in the flour. To this, slowly add a bit of the soup; stir well until smooth. Add this back to the main soup pot and stir well. Repeat this step if necessary to achieve the degree of thickening you prefer. Serve hot with oyster crackers.

Cooks Falls Fish Cakes

3 cups cooked, flaked fish

1 cup mashed potato

$\frac{1}{3}$–$\frac{1}{2}$ cup finely chopped onion

1 large or 2 small eggs

$\frac{1}{2}$ tsp. salt, or to taste

$\frac{1}{4}$ tsp. black pepper, or to taste

Good dash cayenne

1 $\frac{1}{2}$ tsp. chopped fresh dill or $\frac{1}{2}$ tsp. dried

2 T. mayonnaise

2 T. finely chopped sweet pickle

2 T. white wine

Plain dried bread crumbs, preferably from a good-quality
  fresh bread

Butter, preferably clarified

1. Cook whole gutted and gilled fish in a light court bouillon if desired for extra flavor. Otherwise, just poach. Cool slightly. Remove heads, tails, fins, skin, and bones and discard. Flake the meat and measure out 3 cups.

2. Combine the 3 cups of fish meat with all other ingredients except the bread crumbs and butter. If you do use two eggs, add one at a time so that the mixture isn't too soft. I add the mayonnaise and the wine a little at a time for the same reason.

3. Pack some of the mixture into an oiled $\frac{1}{3}$-cup measuring cup, and then tap the mixture out into your hand. Quickly and lightly form the ball into a cake. Repeat until all the mixture has been used.

4. Spread the crumbs out onto a large platter. Bread the cakes on each side by lightly pressing them into the crumbs.

5. Meanwhile, in a large heavy skillet or on a griddle, melt a little butter and turn flame to medium. Sauté the cakes until golden brown on both sides. Adjust the flame down if necessary—the cakes are better when more golden than brown.

Note: I distinctly like the larger quantity of onion, but your taste could differ.

Fig. 5.1 Wild trout in the Catskills. Here are some waters where all or virtually all of the trout you catch will be wild. Not included here are literally hundreds of small mountain streams where wild brook trout (and ocassionally wild brown trout or wild rainbow trout) may be encountered.

WATER	LOCATION	SPECIES	COMMENTS
Main stem of the Delaware River	Sullivan, Delaware Counties	Rainbows, browns	Near Hancock a few stocked browns may be seen. Below Lordville nearly all the trout are wild and all the rainbows in the river are wild.
West Branch Delaware River	Delaware Cty., partially bordering PA	Browns, rainbows	All the rainbows and almost all of the browns are wild.
Mongaup River	Southern Sullivan County	Browns, some brook	No stocking below Mongaup Falls Reservoir. All wild fish. River subject to severe flow fluctuations due to power generation. Section below Rio Reservoir looks very wild.
Rio Reservoir	Southern Sullivan County	Browns	All wild fish, spawned in the Mongaup River. Eagles now nesting in this valley.
Neversink River (gorge)	Sullivan County	Browns, some brook	Most fish in the gorge area thought to be wild. A few stocked browns may drift down from stocked upriver sections.
Neversink Reservoir	Sullivan County	Browns	All wild fish, spawned in the Neversink River and other tribs.
Cannonsville Reservoir	Delaware County	Browns	Wild fish spawned in tributaries. Some stocked browns from heavily stocked upper West Branch Delaware may end up in Cannonsville.
Trout Pond	Delaware County, Town of Colchester	Brook	A walk-in pond (20–25 min.) with shore fishing for wild brook trout. No baitfish allowed. Lies wholly on state land.
Alder Lake	Ulster County, Near Delaware County border	Brook	You can drive to this. Canoes allowed. No baitfish. Lies wholly on state land. Beautiful mountain backdrop.
Catskill Creek	Greene, Albany, and Schoharie Counties	Rainbows	Browns are stocked but all the rainbows are wild and dominate in the upriver sections.
Esopus Creek, above reservoir	Ulster County	Rainbows	I make an exception here. The river is stocked with huge numbers of brown trout but the river has a super population of wild rainbows.

CHAPTER 5

Brookies
and Hemlocks

There was a time only 120 years ago when there were no trout in Catskill rivers. Oh, there was a fish of magnificent coloration: hazy, blackish purple flanks; vermilion dots laid on fields of lavender blue; subtle vermiculations of green; pectoral and ventral fins distinctively edged with white. But this fish, apparently painted by Zeus himself to shame all other fish, was not a trout at all but a char. It was and is, of course, *Salvelinus fontinalis*, "the one that dwells in springs," the native brook trout.

I like to think of the brookie as the ruffed grouse of Catskill rivers. While cackling pheasants and studious brown trout are raised in pens, the grouse and brookie carry on their kind naturally in the hushed, hemlock silence of headwater basins. When all the "good pools" on the river are lined with thousand-dollar fly outfits held by those who must catch 18-inch fish, tiny, moss-lined pools above 2,000 feet remain unseen for seasons at a time. To escape the drone of Route 17 or Route 28, and the even more tedious drone of taxonomical litanies, I ever more frequently climb to these hidden pools. Brookies and hemlocks are perhaps the very essence of the Catskills.

Brook trout, of course, are also raised in pens, but that's not the kind in question here. Here I speak of the 5- to 10-inch "speckles" that live in most of the little tributaries or "rills" in the Catskills. Once common in most of the big rivers in the mountains, at least down to a certain elevation, the brookie has been pushed upstream by the competitive, introduced brown trout and by warmer waters brought on by deforestation. For certain, native brookies are still taken in the main rivers, side by side with the brown. But typically these days, Catskill brook trout fishing means small-water fishing, often very-small-water fishing. For this reason, there are two best times to catch brookies: in early spring, and then later in the season when the brooks are rain swollen. In summer most brook trout streams are very low, and in September they're usually even lower. At these times brookies are terribly skittish, and to catch one you must practice extreme stealth. Even with a careful, stalking approach to water's edge, you're liable to see only fins and tails dashing madly for undercut banks or undercut bridge abutments.

In spring it's easier. The high, roily water will mitigate a clumsy approach, and the relatively unsophisticated brookie will be an easy mark. Then, too, the brookie will be more active in the very cold water of early spring than will the brown. The brook trout seems to be most active at a water temperature of about 55 degrees, while the brown is bounciest at around 58 to 60. Both trout will take both bait and flies right from the gun on April 1. But many times in April, I have caught only brookies in places where I knew browns also lived. I should say that May can also be a fine time to catch brook trout. In fact, in some of the higher, colder watersheds, even brook trout may be sluggish in early spring. In such very cold streams the water may only be in the high 40s by mid- to late May. In early June there's usually enough water in the hills that a rainstorm will quickly swell the headwater tribs. Then you have the best of both worlds: good water flow and temperatures right around the brookie's preference zone. During or after a rainstorm in June is in general a deadly time to take all trout in all places in the Catskills.

Ultralight spinning is an effective tactic for native Catskill brook trout. It's hard to beat a short, $4^1/_2$- to 5-foot spinning stick for poking into tight places. Worms are a top choice, with small garden or corn worms being excellent. What, you don't know what corn worms are? They're a free source of bait, so you should be onto the trick. In April or early May, before the farmer has plowed, corn stubble 6 to 12 inches high will be standing. Yank up one of these stalks and you'll often find pinkish little worms dangling from the now dead roots. They will be more plentiful in some soils than in others, but you should be able to fill your bait can in 30 minutes.

Salted minnows work well at times. Stick to the ones that are around $1^1/_4$ inches in length, and use a size 6 baitholder hook. Push the point of the hook

TOBY McAFEE

A short spinning rod is a good weapon of choice for the small brook trout streams of the Catskills. Approach each potential holding lie with caution, and wear clothing that blends in with your surroundings.

through the eye of the fish, then thread the minnow up and around the shank of the hook. The point should come back out the side of the minnow somewhere in its center. If in rigging this way you've imparted a little curve to the minnow, it will wobble through the water perfectly. With no curve, it will not wobble at all, and it won't look natural. With too much curve, it will spin and twist badly and also won't look natural. The key is to stick to the smaller minnows of $1^{1}/_{4}$ to $1^{3}/_{4}$ inches and to use the right-sized hook for the salted minnow you're using. Twelve inches ahead of the hook, insert a small black barrel swivel. It will be worth your while to purchase a ball-bearing model for this purpose. Then, just above the swivel, add a small split shot. How much shot you need will be determined by the strength of the water flow, but use as little as possible. Sometimes brookies get picky, and then I'll break the minnow in half and fish the head or tail dead-drift in the current. I especially like to use salted minnows in the bigger brook trout streams, in the hope of also connecting with a nice brown.

Without doubt, the deadliest medicine in these fast, rocky brooks is a small revolving-blade spinner. It can be cast upstream where the water is a bit deeper, or across and down in somewhat thinner water. Be sure to keep the hook points razor sharp, but even with that precaution you'll still drop a lot of these small trout.

Sometimes, Catskill headwater streams are overgrown, and this makes the use of most lures quite difficult. One good tactic is to use the smallest floating Rapala or similar lure you can buy. Let it drift down from your position, then twitch it as it passes what you think to be a good holding lie. By the same token, you can work a small wobbler or even a spinner in a downstream manner. Flip the little lure, close the bail, and then let the lure hang in the current. Move your rod from side to side to cover the width of the stream. If you dangle your lure in front of a trout's nose long enough, he may eventually pounce on it out of aggravation.

Don't judge a brook trout brook from the road. Get into your hip boots and start wading and casting. I'm willing to bet you'll discover that there's more holding water than you thought. You'll probably also discover that there are more trout than you thought.

Fly-fishing can be practiced anywhere, but fly-casting is only possible on the bigger brook trout waters. What hatches will you encounter? It's a fact that as you head downstream in almost any watershed, you'll pick up new species while also retaining the ones encountered farther upstream (there's naturally a limit to this). To reverse this thinking, as you head upstream there will be fewer species—flies, minnows, and other aquatic life-forms. My experience has been that minnow life is poor in most headwater Catskill trout streams, though the slimy sculpin is one species that may be seen upstream. What I have seen most often have been stoneflies—which makes sense, given that the four-winged *Plecoptera* species like fast, well-oxygenated water. Caddisflies are also important upstream insects. Often, they will dominate the headwater picture. Remember, though, that as a matter of general principle, brook trout are known for hitting bright and often nonimitative attractor flies such as the Royal Coachman, Grizzly King, Professor, Montreal, and so on.

When fly-fishing upstream, you might think a short rod to be right on cue. Sometimes that's true. At other times you may need a longer rod to help you "dap." To dap means to gently drop your fly onto a likely piece of water without any real casting motion. When a small brook is low, you may have to dap, often as you reach precariously over the old beaver dam you're half standing on. While doing this I've set the hook and had a 5- or 6-inch brookie come sailing through the air like a tuna and land on the ground right by my feet.

Here are a few additional random tips on fishing these sparkling little rills.

Look for some of the best fish at the bridge pools, which are often some of the deepest pools on many of these brooks. If there's a pipe under the bridge, nice-sized brookies may actually hold in the pipe. Approach these better pools with extreme caution. If you spot a nice fish but can't fool it, wait for another time—perhaps a rainy day, with the brook swollen—and have another go at your prize. Plan your strategy well. Make that first cast count. Stay low to the ground. Wear drab clothing.

Be on the watch for new ponds created by beavers on side channels of your favorite creek. This is a great place to drop a dry fly, which will disturb the tiny pond far less than would a spinning lure. Approach such ponds with the utmost care, and once you're within casting distance, stop and sit down for 10 minutes. Then make your cast from just behind the front line of vegetation if that's feasible.

Try your chosen brook after a good rainstorm in mid- to late September. You might be electrified by the jolt of a big brownie moving up in anticipation of spawning. In a few watersheds, large rainbows are possible in the headwaters, especially in early spring.

There's a good side and a bad side to hunting up brookie streams. On the downside, fewer public easements exist on the headwater streams; more effort has been expended in obtaining these to stretches of the bigger, more popular waters. On the plus side, good brookie streams are often higher up in the mountains, and in the Catskills, the higher you go, the greater the chance of finding state forest lands.

One erroneous assumption is that you have to be far up into the mountains to catch wild brook trout. In all the Catskill counties (but Greene least of all), there are small meadow streams that harbor wild brookies and—since few of these are stocked—sometimes only wild brookies. The often narrow channel, the drooping vegetation, and the presence of springs help keep these brooks cold enough for brook trout. Some are surprisingly deep despite their narrowness. Some are very difficult to get at because of swampy conditions. Standard topographical maps are essential for exploring these often overlooked meadow streams.

On the Trail of the 16-Inch Native

The brook is born at 1,800 feet, in a little headwater swamp right near my old hunting camp. It's not much to look at in summer, yet even in August it gurgles along fresh and cool, and it gives welcome refuge to the trout where it joins the Beaver Kill.

As with so many Catskill brooks, the deepest pool is by a bridge. The trout there are skittish in the extreme, and when you peer over you usually see only tails darting madly into the undermined abutments. This time, though, I tried a new approach. I parked my car 50 yards away and literally stalked up to the brook, a step at a time. Ever so carefully I approached the bridge, and when I slowly leaned over an electrical charge shot up my spine. There were about six brookies visible, and I guessed the largest one at 14 inches. Allowing for refraction and exaggeration, the biggest one still had to be 13 inches long, and that's a very big brookie from such a tiny stream.

It's a worthy challenge: stalking the largest native brookies you can find! How big do they grow in the Catskills? Probing that question led me to some fascinating data.

Native Catskill brook trout are genetically limited to a three-year life span. Only 3 or 4 in 100 make it to four years, and a five-year-old fish would be extraordinarily rare. But they aren't limited in how much they can eat within that life span. If the conditions are particularly good—good feed and a longer growing season brought on by unusually favorable temperatures—Catskill brookies can and will pack a lot of growth into a short life.

Theodore Gordon once said that he never saw a brookie bigger than 14

*A wild brook trout of about 13 inches, taken from a
small Catskill pond above 2,000 feet.*

inches in the Catskills. Nonetheless, a few natives this size and a little bigger
do turn up in the brooks. For example, there have been reports of brook trout
as large as 17 inches below the Neversink dam. Brookies of 16 to 18 inches
have also reportedly been taken from the upper West Branch of the Neversink, which is not a tailwater but pretty much the same stream that existed
in Gordon's time.

But the best chance for a true 16-inch native occurs in the ponds and
lakes of the Catskills. Both Rondout and Neversink Reservoirs are very cold
and clean, and from each, oversized brookies of at least 16 to 18 inches have
been taken. Not too long ago there was an unconfirmed report of a 20-inch
brookie caught in Neversink. Such brook trout are certainly rare in these impoundments, but they do occur. Possibilities for a 16-inch brook trout also
exist in Pepacton Reservoir.

Catskill ponds can also offer the promise of a jumbo brook trout, if you
can find a good pond. There are essentially two types: beaver ponds, and
other ponds.

A "flow-through" beaver pond is one located directly on a stream. Conditions here, notably water temperatures, will not usually be different enough
from the stream itself to cultivate larger brook trout. Some big browns can

develop in this type of pond, though. The other type of beaver pond is one more or less isolated from a flowing brook, perhaps one that's spring fed. Here food may be better and temperatures more moderate: warmer in spring and fall, maybe even open in winter, and cooler in summer. Such an ideal environment with its longer growing season can indeed harbor brook trout of at least 2 pounds or about 16 to 17 inches. Such ponds are usually very small, often only 1/4 acre or less! They used to be rare in the Catskills, but a burgeoning beaver population is creating hundreds of new little ponds on watersheds all across the mountains.

In the non-beaver-dam ponds of the Catskills swim perhaps the largest brook trout. One pond that I won't name occasionally yields wild brook trout up to about 18 inches and possibly a hair bigger. In Sullivan County's Crystal Lake, anglers have taken wild brook trout of up to at least 17 inches. This town of Fremont pond was reclaimed—poisoned off to remove all fish—then stocked with Catskill-strain brookies imported from the headwaters of the Beaver Kill. Food here is plentiful, and the brookies thrived and reproduced, with many 14-inch fish taken and six-month-old fish averaging an amazing 8 inches. Then smallmouth bass got into Crystal and so the DEC had to start all over again. I have no word on how the pond is doing in its new incarnation.

The late Bill Kelly was a DEC regional fisheries manager, and he provided some of the information for this chapter. He made some of the most impressive catches I have heard of, including a doubleheader he once took from a private Catskill pond. While fishing his usual tandem wet flies he took, on the same cast, two brookies totaling 31 inches in length: one 17 inches, the other 14 inches.

I never got to ask Bill if these were stocked fish or truly outstanding Catskill natives.

CHAPTER 6

Variety in the
Lake District

While ponds are numerous in the Catskills, lakes are not. The one real exception is the southeastern two-thirds of Sullivan County, the area that I call the Lake District. Some might argue that this hilly and often deeply fissured region, south and east of Route 52, isn't even in the Catskills. However, the geologist's definition of the Catskills—"a maturely dissected part of the Allegheny Plateau," as author Alf Evers relates it—makes the boundaries of this resort region so amorphous that no one is likely to take me to task on it.

Some of the dozens of lakes found here are natural, while others are natural lakes that were artificially raised. But the largest and most productive ones are man-made, and most were formed on the Mongaup River system. The primary game fish present in the Lake District is the largemouth bass. Smallmouth bass and chain pickerel also provide fine challenges, with the pickerel being the more widespread. Some very large chain pickerel are taken here. Long and thin Swinging Bridge Reservoir plays host to the good-eating walleye, a species that's rumored to also exist in one or two other area lakes. Lake trout and brown trout are found in only a few of these lakes, and while they are largely stocked fish, one important reservoir has all wild trout. Panfish such as yellow perch, crappies, and bluegills are abundant.

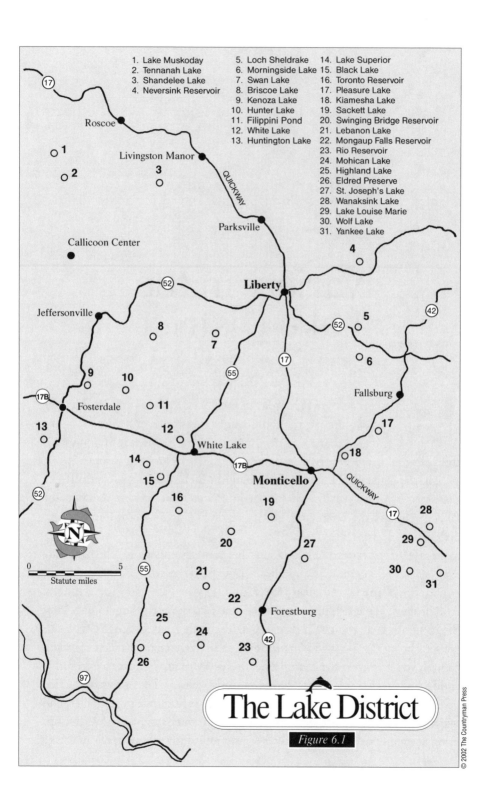

1. Lake Muskoday
2. Tennanah Lake
3. Shandelee Lake
4. Neversink Reservoir
5. Loch Sheldrake
6. Morningside Lake
7. Swan Lake
8. Briscoe Lake
9. Kenoza Lake
10. Hunter Lake
11. Filippini Pond
12. White Lake
13. Huntington Lake
14. Lake Superior
15. Black Lake
16. Toronto Reservoir
17. Pleasure Lake
18. Kiamesha Lake
19. Sackett Lake
20. Swinging Bridge Reservoir
21. Lebanon Lake
22. Mongaup Falls Reservoir
23. Rio Reservoir
24. Mohican Lake
25. Highland Lake
26. Eldred Preserve
27. St. Joseph's Lake
28. Wanaksink Lake
29. Lake Louise Marie
30. Wolf Lake
31. Yankee Lake

The Lake District

Figure 6.1

The bass fishing is good enough here to have inspired the organization of a couple of active bass fishing clubs, which have staged bass tournaments on many Sullivan County lakes, especially Swan Lake, White Lake, and Swinging Bridge Reservoir. A good tip for gathering information on this part of the Catskills would be to read the outdoor columns in area newspapers. The *River Reporter* in Callicoon and the *Sullivan County Democrat* in Monticello are two. Grab these and other newspapers whenever you're in the mountains and you'll be amazed at how much you'll pick up on local fishing.

In this chapter I've presented brief introductions to eight noteworthy lakes or reservoirs in the Lake District. A ninth, the Basher Kill, is just outside the Lake District. On all these, there is at least some public access. There are many, many other lakes in the district—some named and roughly located on figure 6.1—but a high percentage of these are private, even though some limited access is possible on many. Even on the "public lakes" I'll discuss, access situations vary greatly and are often a bit sticky.

Contour maps of many of these lakes are available from the Region 3 office of the DEC, the address for which is provided on page 211. Especially in the southerly part of Sullivan County, main roads are scarce and in some cases you positively must have a good road map to avoid getting lost. Topographical maps would be useful for exploring the Neversink River and the Mongaup River system. Finally, you might want to contact—if not join, through a member club—the 6,000-member Sullivan County Sportsmen, a federation of organizations.

In keeping with the spirit of this book, I've selected stillwaters that offer a more or less tranquil experience. Electric motors are permissible on all of these, but gasoline motors on only a few, including the first one to come under discussion.

Toronto Reservoir

At 860 acres, Toronto is second in size in the Lake District only to Swinging Bridge. One of a string of hydroelectric reservoirs created on the Mongaup system, it was formerly under the wing of the Orange & Rockland utility company and is now owned and operated by Mirant. The general public is allowed to fish here without any special permit, and all seasons and regulations are statewide. While a cartopper with a small motor would be appropriate, there are no restrictions on either boat or motor size. Some anglers do bring trailered boats here—bass boat sized, not cabin cruiser sized. On week-

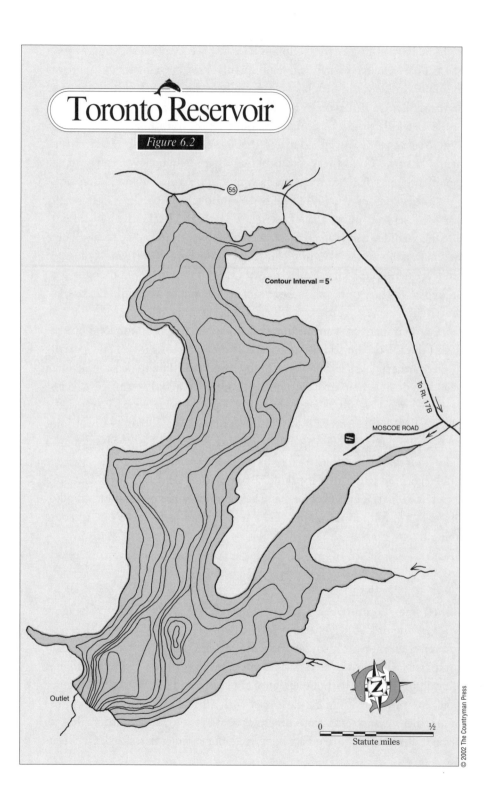

Toronto Reservoir

Figure 6.2

Contour Interval = 5'

55

To Rt. 17B

MOSCOE ROAD

Outlet

0   ½
Statute miles

days and in spring and autumn, angler use is not excessive, and Toronto offers a reasonably pleasant experience with plenty of water to roam.

Toronto has a maximum depth of 85 feet, but most of it is much shallower. Rather severe water-level fluctuations adversely affect the habitat. Because of its particular oxygen-temperature profile, Toronto is not suitable for trout. While a few may be found, this is primarily a warm-water lake, with largemouth bass and pickerel predominant. Some extremely large chain pickerel have done their head-shaking act at Toronto's surface, witness the 8-pound, 1-ounce state-record pickerel caught here in 1965.

There is an unusual restriction at Toronto. Approximately one-third of the reservoir is totally off limits, boat and shore, as the exclusive fishing rights to it are owned by the Iroquois Sportsman's Club. I have heard that their water is delineated by marker buoys.

There has not been a recent DEC survey here, so it's hard to speak authoritatively about the quality of the fishing. In the last survey, quite some years ago, the largemouth bass and pickerel were rated as fairly good but not great. The severe drawdowns are likely to depress these highly littoral species.

The best-known access point to this lake is off Moscoe Road. If you're heading west on Route 17B from Monticello, look for Route 55 south just past White Lake. Take that left and go about 2 miles. Moscoe Road will be on your left. Take that left and after a mile or less you'll come to a back cove on the lake. You should find adequate parking and a place to leave your trailer if you're using one. The shoreline should facilitate the easy launching of a small boat. I visited this locale at a time when the water was down—a common scenario—and people were having no problem putting in, although the launch is not a spectacular one

Another launch site is near the dam. I'm told that you can reach this via a local road, but I haven't yet visited this site, and the maps I have of the area do not make the avenue of access clear.

Lake Superior

This is not the one that's 1,333 feet deep and holds a tenth of the world's fresh water. It's actually a small Sullivan County lake that takes up only 186 acres, but I've included it here because the access is good and the bass fishing can be, too.

The lake and its banks form a park, and while the park is under the aegis of the Palisades Interstate Park Commission, it's administered by Sullivan

Two canoeists about to put in at Lake Superior. This state park offers largemouth bass, pickerel, and panfish. Note shore casters casting into the lily pads that grow thick at this end of the lake.

County, which leases it. There's a small bathing beach that's popular in summer, and there are tables and grills for picnicking. There is a modest entrance fee of a couple of bucks, but anglers who come before 9 A.M. can enter for free. It's open to fishing from sunrise to sunset, though the word is that local enforcement personnel do not disturb anglers who are still casting away after dark. As you pull into the parking lot off the local road that connects Routes 55 and 17B, bear to the right and you'll find a small launching area and parking lot just for fishermen. All you need is a small cartopper of 12 feet, or a canoe. They also rent sturdy, 12-foot semi-V aluminum rowboats here in-season at the rate of $6 per hour or $20 for four hours. You may bring an electric trolling motor and use it on your boat or theirs, but gas outboards are disallowed.

The important game fish here are largemouth bass and pickerel. The largemouths are reasonably abundant, with 12- to 17-inchers predominant. Larger specimens are boated but reportedly not common. As of recently, largemouth bass have been stocked by the park, and I've also heard that some smallmouths were stocked by the local federation of sportsmen's clubs, although it really doesn't look like a smallmouth lake.

One lucky angler took a pickerel that stretched the tape out to an impressive 30 inches.

Superior is a pretty, very bassy-looking lake with thick lily pads found in at least one of its coves. Connected to Superior by a shallow channel is Chestnut Ridge Pond, reputed to hold a few nice bass. The gentleman running the boat concession tells me that when the water level is up you can get into Chestnut Ridge with a canoe, but during low water it's difficult.

I'm not averse to fishing a body of water that other recreationists use, as long as those other uses are harmonious with and not harmful to the environment. Superior is a small, cozy park, and the bathers use only one small edge of the lake. It would be an excellent place to bring family members who can swim and picnic while you fish. Take a dip yourself after an invigorating morning out on the water.

White Lake

White Lake is one of only two lakes I know of in the Catskills to contain lake trout, the other being Rondout Reservoir. Lake trout were apparently first stocked here in the 1930s, and some natural reproduction is said to occur.

This is a small lake, and it's overwhelmed by power watercraft during the summer. You can easily cover it with a cartopper and an electric motor, but don't try telling that to the summer and permanent residents whose homes ring the lake almost completely. I include it only because of the ice-fishing possibilities.

As you can see from the map, White Lake is nearly split in two by facing points of land. This popular hard-water destination is 288 acres and has a maximum depth of 85 feet. There are some very steep drop-offs, mainly in the south basin. There also are considerable shallows, making for a productive two-story fishery. Public access is guaranteed via a DEC ramp, as shown in figure 6.3. Ice fishermen who park on Route 17B or on local side streets and walk out to fish are seldom bothered. As I've said, many of the houses on the lake are second homes and are vacant in winter. As noisy as the lake is in the warm months, the softness of a snowy winter day seems to blot out most human indiscretions. But then, just when you're sitting on your bucket and starting to feel reposeful, the snowmobiles and ice boats come out.

I do most of my ice fishing in southeastern New York, but since White often freezes up sooner this is sometimes my first destination. I've gotten out

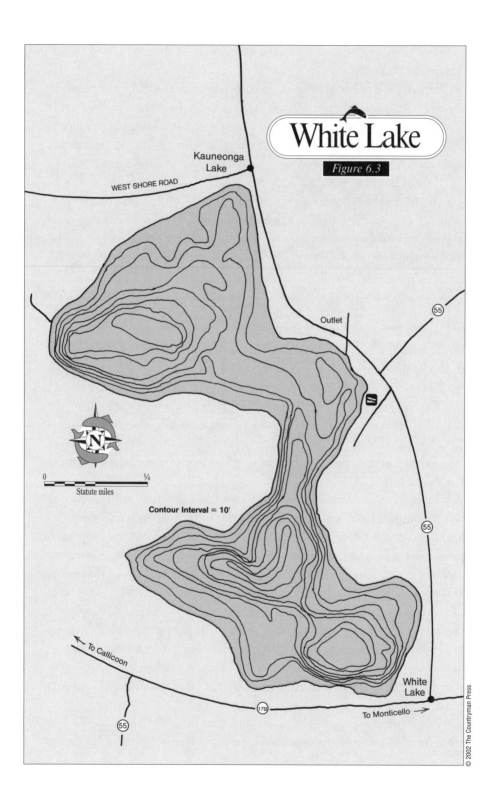

White Lake

Figure 6.3

Kauneonga Lake

WEST SHORE ROAD

Outlet

55

N

0   ¼
Statute miles

Contour Interval = 10'

55

To Callicoon

White Lake

17B

To Monticello →

55

© 2002 The Countryman Press

here as early as Christmas Eve, but I know in some years anglers beat that by up to three weeks.

Each year the DEC stocks brown trout (5,000 in a recent year) and lake trout (1,600 in that same year). Holdover is very good, and 5-pound specimens aren't all that uncommon. Browns may be kept at any size, but lakers must be 15 inches. The take limit is five trout, of which three may be lakers, but you'll be doing well to catch one nice trout in a day's ice fishing.

As for the warm-water species, White Lake was once principally a largemouth lake, but the DEC tells me that the Sullivan County Sportsman's Federation put in some smallmouths some years ago (with permission) and now smallies are established, too. Bass fishing for the knowledgeable is quite good, and tournaments are held here. Pickerel are present in some very good sizes.

Some very large lakers were taken here in the past, up to at least 15 pounds. In recent years the lake trout fishery has tailed off. Tests have shown very poor late-summer oxygen levels, and that may have something to do with it. Browns now predominate.

The serious angler who doesn't ice fish will want to get out in spring or fall, or very early in the morning in summer.

Vassmer's is a store located right on White Lake, a few miles north of Route 17B. They have bait and some tackle plus food and drinks. I usually call them in the early season to see if the ice is good yet.

Mongaup Valley Wildlife Management Area

The often ugly constructs of people turned golden about 20 years ago when a bald eagle apparently heading south for the winter looked down (with his eagle eye?) at the Mongaup River and said to himself, "What a minute— aren't those dead fish floating down there?" The dam, the turbines, the sawbellies—it all would have fallen into place for our feathered opportunist had he been able to think it through. The bird came back the next winter with (we can imagine) a few cousins and aunts and uncles and before you knew it, this lightly developed and rugged river valley had become the most important eagle wintering site in New York State. Perhaps 25 now spend at least part of the winter here, and at least a few pairs are nesting. The state *had* to take steps to protect the setting in which this small miracle was taking place, and the result was new land purchases and easements that, when added to existing ones, helped create the Mongaup Valley Wildlife Management Area, some 16,000 contiguous acres of public land or land to which there is some public access. It is fair to state that it isn't only the Mongaup that's attracting eagles; the real-life feathered incarnations of our national symbol are now nesting on the Delaware River (they've long wintered there), on certain of the Catskill reservoirs, and even in the lower Hudson Valley.

There must be at least a dozen different types of signs located within the boundary of the management area. Some tell you where you can and cannot be, others when you can and cannot be there, and still others what you can and cannot do. Then there are "Restricted Areas" within otherwise open territories, rod-and-gun club signs, regular old posted signs, power company signs, signs related to access and boating, signs about the special releases for kayakers, and illegal signs put up by people who own land in the area and try to con you into not entering where you're really allowed to. Part of this almost comical situation stems from the fact that so many different groups have a legal interest in the valley—it is not simply one big parcel of state land.

With the exception of a couple of eagle viewing points, this entire WMA is completely closed to the public from December 1 to March 31 to protect the easily disturbed raptors. During the other eight months, anglers can take advantage of some of the most interesting stillwater fishing in the Lake District. The small amount of viable trout stream mileage that exists here sees some coverage in chapter 7. Here, I'll discuss four considerably large lakes that lie wholly or partially within Mongaup Valley Wildlife Management Area.

The northern tip of the management area touches part of Swinging Bridge, but don't judge the area by that lake, which I have excluded from this edition because of the extreme disturbance there from high-horsepower motors. When you move west and south from Swinging Bridge you leave behind the houseboats and the jetskis and truly step into another world. Other chapters have encouraged exploration on lesser-known streams. Here in the Mongaup Valley you can actually do a little exploring to stillwaters.

I will need to be specific with directions here, since a good map of the management area does not yet exist and even some good road maps do not show these dirt roads.

Route 43 is a main road (for this area) that links Forestburgh in the east and Eldred in the west. Put your finger on the map. Immediately to the east of where Route 43 crosses Mongaup Falls Reservoir is a gated dirt road that will lead to your first destination. Sometimes the gate isn't open until May 1, but after that, and up to early November, it should be open and passable. Should you find yourself here in November, don't attempt this road if snow has fallen unless you have a four-wheel drive. For that matter, don't attempt this road at any time if you own an especially low-slung car.

Heading north on this road, you'll be paralleling the section of the Mongaup River that flows out of Swinging Bridge and into Mongaup Falls. This piece is mentioned in chapter 7. Cross the little wooden bridge and then, instead of turning right toward the main Swinging Bridge dam and the power plant, turn left and curl up and around a fairly steep hill. Six-tenths of a mile after that turn you'll come to a fork. Bear left, and you'll almost immediately see a minor dam and outflow of Swinging Bridge Reservoir. There is no actual road here; you'll be crossing a remarkable field of reddish igneous rock—lava, of a sort—and you may have to drive through a little water. This may not be crossable at times; I don't know. Looking to your left, you'll see that you're on the eastern edge of a spectacular canyon. Past this point you must go about another 0.5 mile before you see a parking spot for one car on your right, just before a locked gate. If a vehicle is parked there, back up a few dozen yards to another larger parking spot on the opposite side of this dirt road. The gate, unmarked by any signs at this time, is the entrance point to Cliff Lake, our aim for today. It's about a 0.5-mile walk to the lake. You can't drive to it, but some anglers have brought in small cartoppers and canoes on dollies. This is legal, and electric motors are also legal, but gas motors are forbidden. The walk in is level, but when you get to the lake you must curl up and around a moderate incline. This is a factor, though two strong anglers pulling a canoe or small boat on wheels can do it. When you get up to the lake, you'll have to take a narrow trail across a little wooden bridge. Then, very quickly you'll see a somewhat nondescript but marked put-in point in a small cove. The reward for all this huffing and puffing can be considerable—you may have the lake to yourself.

Cliff Lake, long off limits to public fishing, is long and narrow and extremely scenic, with only the big ugly dam and a string of buoys in front of it seeming out of place. It's ringed almost completely by native white pines, with a few red maples. In sunny spots, as by the dam, you'll find succulent red raspberry, lowbush blueberry, yarrow, and sweet fern. When I visited in early July the lake was down about 7 feet, which made shore casting feasible. Even with the lowered lake level you're standing on a good pitch as you cast. With the lake at full pool, it would be hard to imagine how you could effectively fish from shore. But maybe it's almost always down a few feet. Be that as it may, one state official told me that shore casting is technically limited to only a certain portion of Cliff Lake, perhaps another good reason to do the aforementioned huffing and puffing.

This warm-water lake has both largemouth and smallmouth bass, and pickerel. With the extremely light pressure it gets, the fishing may be very good, but there was no way for me to confirm this. A lake is not necessarily very productive simply because it's remote.

Just as I got back to the car on the way out, I thought about how isolated a spot it was. Wouldn't you know it that no sooner did I have that thought than up roars a big pickup truck with half the senior class riding in back. The eight or nine shirtless mules were full of themselves, but essentially benign. But I thought later: What if they hadn't been?

Out of this experience come two suggestions for Cliff Lake: Fish with someone, and don't leave a lot of stuff visible in your car.

Lebanon Lake lies just to the west of Cliff Lake. It's much larger and more rounded in shape. A road does come near it, but it's still wild looking, and its banks are undeveloped. There is reported to be some excellent pickerel and yellow perch fishing here. I've often heard of Lebanon in reference to ice fishing, one of my favorite activities. The property owners give out a limited number of permits yearly by lottery, and they go quickly. Given the changes of ownership in some of the properties within Mongaup Valley, I was unable to fully plumb the Lebanon Lake access picture; I leave that task to the interested reader.

Mongaup Falls Reservoir lies between larger Swinging Bridge and Rio Reservoirs. It doesn't have quite the stunning stark quality of Rio, but its banks are similarly undeveloped, and the setting here in this quiet corner of Sullivan County is extremely peaceful. Once again, small boats or canoes with electric motors are permitted, and there is a good launch as well as plenty of parking a few hundred yards to the east of where Route 43 crosses the lake. An official eagle viewing station is located on the lake near the southeast corner of the bridge.

About 1,500 yearling browns are stocked here annually, and some get to be at least 6 or 7 pounds. Because of the extreme fluctuations in the flow from Swinging Bridge—remember, this outflow is used for power generation—and the generally anoxic condition of that flow, the possibility for natural reproduction of browns would seem to be very limited. But holdover in the reservoir is good, and this 120-acre lake does have some devoted followers.

Shore anglers, many of whom live in nearby communities, fish the deep pool that is also the long inlet area of the lake at the Route 43 bridge. One fisherman I met says he takes more than a few good browns at this easily accessed spot. I caught some small largemouth bass here, and saw many panfish in the shallows.

Farther down on the Mongaup River system is Rio Reservoir. This beautiful, wild-looking, 460-acre impoundment is also used for power generation, and it has a reputation for big brown trout. Rio is much clearer than its upstream sister, Swinging Bridge, which filters out the murkiness. Biologists call this a "nutrient trap." Between the clearer water and the much prettier scenery, Rio provides a beautiful backdrop for a day's fishing.

The deepest part is 95 feet, while the average depth is about 38 feet. The banks are generally quite steep and there are numerous drop-offs and rocky points.

Rio is very much suited for trout, and although the DEC doesn't stock them, browns of 10 pounds and better have been taken. These are obviously the progeny of fish spawning in the Mongaup River and perhaps other tributaries. I met someone who fishes here three times a week, and he speaks of largemouth bass in excellent sizes and numbers, with one good spot being near where Lake Metauque's outlet enters. There are also smallmouths, and indeed, you can easily see that the habitat might suit both species. For example, the north end of the lake is quite shallow and narrow, and you need only a rowboat or a canoe to fish this water. Anglers seeking more mobility bring small boats with electric motors, and put in at the DEC trailer-boat launch on Plank Road very close to the inlet on the east bank. Secondarily, you can hand-launch at another DEC parking lot at the southwest corner of the dam. This simple launch is steep, but if all you're using is a 12-foot cartopper, and you're with a buddy, you can handle it.

As with Mongaup Falls Reservoir, no gas motors are allowed and no special boating permit is required. Just pull up with your boat, a valid state fishing license, a fishing pole, and a couple of turkey sandwiches in the cooler.

General statewide regulations and seasons are in effect, and the public may fish here from April through November. Ice fishing is not allowed. Study the signs posted around the lake so that you steer clear of restricted areas.

On a recent visit here, I was standing on shore no more than five minutes before someone pointed out an eagle in a tree on the opposite shore. Within minutes of that, its mate appeared and landed in the tall, scruffy pine. We then heard a ruckus, which may have been the fussing of the eaglets being fed.

At the time of this writing, the final plan for the Mongaup Valley

Wildlife Management Area is still being written. These lands and waters are a tremendous resource for all outdoors lovers, but the above-stated conditions, regulations, and opportunities are highly subject to change.

The Basher Kill

Is the Basher Kill a stream, a lake, or a marsh? In truth, it's a little of each, and since it offers such an unusual angling experience, I include it even though it lies just outside the Catskills.

It rises as a regular old trout stream in the southeast corner of Sullivan County, near Phillipsport. It curls around and somewhat parallels Route 209 for about 4 miles, just skirting the village of Wurtsboro. Recently, I stopped and looked off the bridge over the stream at the eastern edge of Wurtsboro. Trout! Nice ones. This is not state stocked—clubs may stock it—but there are several miles of stream above the marsh, where those who savor the out-of-the-way might want to look for some access. I did see posted signs at the bridge. Note that there is also a bit of stream below that bridge, before you get to the marsh. When I fished this deep, slow, meandering bit of stream recently, using little pull-offs on South Road east of the marsh, I expected a 14-inch brookie to belt my fly at any moment. None did, on that day.

Just below or southwest of Wurtsboro, it falls into the well-known Basher Kill (also spelled Bashakill) marsh, home to beavers and much else.

A short way below the Route 17 bridge, the Basher Kill widens and becomes more lakelike, and here it is protected and preserved within the 2,468-acre Bashakill State Wildlife Management Area. The slow-moving lakelike river, the surrounding marsh, and the uplands around the marsh are open to both hunting and fishing as well as general nature study and observation. The DEC has created parking areas and boat launches for sportsmen and other visitors. You must park, launch, and take out in designated spots only. The Region 3 office of the DEC has a combination map–brochure that will help you locate these points, and tell you more about the marsh.

Really, when anglers speak about the Basher Kill it's the 7-mile-long lake section. The water averages only about 11 feet deep, so canoes or small cartoppers are in order, but I recommend a canoe. Gas motors are not allowed, but electric trolling motors are; use a weed guard. Oars or paddles are a must to get you into places where even the electric won't take you. After spring, heavy vegetation forms. Sturdy tackle and line of 10- to 15-pound test gives you a chance of wrestling that hawg out of his biotic fortress.

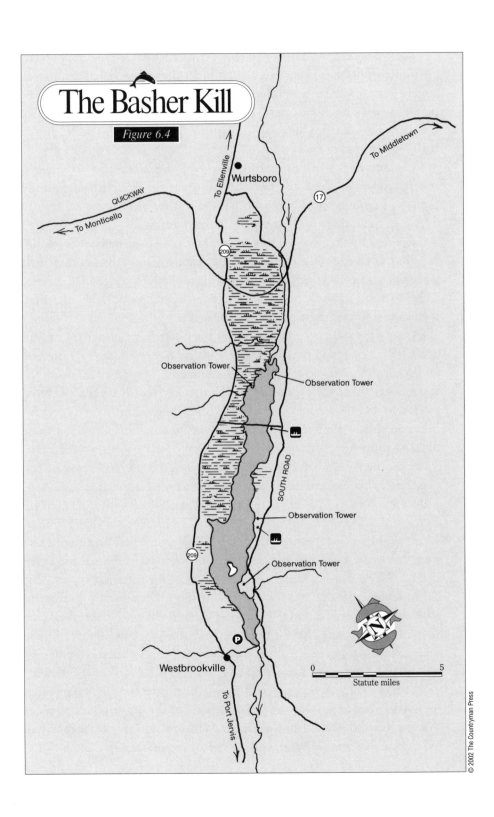

The Basher Kill

Figure 6.4

To Ellenville

To Middletown

Wurtsboro

QUICKWAY

17

To Monticello

209

Observation Tower

Observation Tower

SOUTH ROAD

Observation Tower

209

Observation Tower

P

Westbrookville

To Port Jervis

0   5
Statute miles

Most people come here for largemouths, which are in good supply. The chain pickerel is the other popular and plentiful game fish. Also hiding among the arrow arum, purple loosestrife, and other aquatic and water's-edge plants are eels, bullheads, perch, crappies, bluegills, and a strange finfish known as a bowfin. See the essay in chapter 3 for more on this exotic throwback to the dinosaur days.

Definitely bring some buzzbaits and some weedless surface or shallow-running spoons or crankbaits. Weedless worms or jigs, or jig and pig, will also produce. In summer you'll probably have to seek out the narrow channels to find open water that's not completely choked with weeds.

Local people say that the bass fishing here can be top notch. Substantiation for this may be seen in the DEC law that pertains to the Basher Kill: It is the only water in the area open year-round for both pickerel and black bass. This law stems not only from the good populations available, but also from the fact that summertime fishing is so difficult.

One of the most rewarding views in the Catskills is not in the Catskills at all. It's the one from the Haven Road bridge, where you can gaze both up and down this glorious wetland, the Shawangunk Mountains in which the marsh is nestled providing a fitting backdrop. This is surely the place to bring binoculars and field guides, as well as a fishing pole. Don't forget insect repellent and long-sleeved garments to protect against the bugs, or go those times of year when there are fewer bugs.

Float the Basher Kill marsh sometime soon. You won't be sorry.

Huntington Lake

This roughly teardrop-shaped, fertile, 100-acre lake lies on the extreme western edge of the Lake District, and even farther out of the mainstream of Catskill fishing than some of these other lakes. Eighty percent of its shoreline has residential development, and there are motorboats docked in front of some of these. I will almost always avoid a small lake where motorboats are allowed, but I include Huntington because it offers that uncommon wintertime poke at a trout, and also because I like the unpretentious community, Huntington Lake, in which it is housed.

The 35 feet of depth is apparently enough to foster the cold water that in turn allows the oxygen-loving trout to ride out the hot summer months. While it's doubtful that there's any natural reproduction of trout, there is said to be some excellent holdover. In the season just past, the DEC put in 2,200

*Largemouth bass are normally sluggish for most of the winter,
but they do pop up through the ice from time to time. They must be
returned this time of year except in the Basher Kill.*

yearling browns. The department stopped stocking rainbows a number of years ago because of the appearance of alewives. While alewives and rainbows are often not a good mix, alewives seem to have improved the brown trout fishing, and some amazing specimens have come out of this small lake in recent years. Largemouth bass and panfish lend spice to the action.

If you bring your own boat, the official and well-marked DEC launch site is about two-thirds of the way down the lake on the west bank. Shore-based anglers and ice anglers may also utilize the parking next to the launch.

If you are ice fishing and the weather has been especially unkind, pop into Pete's tavern for a blood warmer and a sandwich, as well as a perfect lakeside view. Watch your tip-ups from here?

Catskill Ice Fishing

It was snowing. If it's the Catskills and it's between November and March, it will seem as if it's always snowing. Maybe not heavy snow, but constant gray skies and flurries. I've often wondered if this might be because this corner of the Catskills is just on the edge of lake-effect snow from Lake Ontario.

Earlier, it had been 12 degrees at the Monticello diner. The flakes bit into our faces relentlessly, so we turned our backs to the fierce wind that was rolling through the cut on White Lake.

Can you imagine a person's first lake trout being only 7 inches long? It's the great char of the great depths, yet there I was, sheepishly holding this bait-sized specimen while someone sarcastically snapped a photo. Jimmy Booth and I caught and threw back three more sublegal-sized lakers and then, just as I was getting discouraged, two young men walked by pulling their ice sled. On top of the sled were an 18-incher and a 21-incher, and they were beautiful fish! Later, at about 6:30 in the evening, my phone rang. It was an Irish fellow from Yonkers whom I had met on the lake that day. He'd stuck it out and at 4:30 had taken a 6-pound laker. I'd told Jimmy you have to fish that last hour of daylight, but his cold feet had pushed us off the lake at 4 P.M.

In the Catskills, trout capital of the East, there is surprisingly little ice fishing for trout. Of course you can't ice fish any of the streams for trout. And the watershed reservoirs, where the bigger trout live, are off limits to ice fishing. Thus, it's some of the Catskills' less heralded species that finally get a little recognition in winter.

The smaller Catskill ponds freeze as early as November; a friend once saw a pond near the top of Peekamoose Mountain frozen solid on November 1. Generally, though, there is little angler activity until mid-December. In a good cold year, most of the good-sized Catskill lakes are locked up by Christmas. In a warmer year, it may be early January, but there will always be some safe ice after that—a guarantee I couldn't make for my home waters in Westchester and Putnam Counties. Again depending on temperature, ice fishing may continue through the productive month of March, with a few diehards continuing into early April. The closing of the pickerel season after March 15 generally puts a damper on things, though.

Despite the above comments, you can take wintertime trout in the Catskills. In the Lake District as defined in this chapter, you have White Lake and Huntington Lake. There are also a few small ponds scattered about the Catskills and discussed or listed in other parts of the text.

How about bass? You have exactly one choice: the Basher Kill, discussed in this chapter. It's the only area water where black bass may legally be kept (and therefore fished for) in winter. Watch out for thin ice, as the Basher Kill is really a slow-moving river, not a lake! Don't ice fish here unless you're experienced, and even then exercise extreme caution.

Chain pickerel is a hard-water staple in the Catskills and beyond. They are normally very cooperative in winter. On the Basher Kill, just mentioned, pickerel as well as bass may be taken home 12 months of the year. Pickerel are common in most Lake District waters, and in quite a few waters in Orange and Ulster Counties. In the Lake District, chain pickerel reach outstanding sizes in some waters.

Walleyes can be taken through the ice on the larger pools of the main stem of the Delaware. This is a long-standing tradition in the huge pool at Narrowsburg, and it's sometimes also done at Lackawaxen and Pond Eddy. The walleye season is the same as the pickerel season: You can keep five legal-sized walleyes per day up to and including March 15.

"Sucker hooking" is an old tradition on the Delaware, and on parts of the Susquehanna, too. This unusual winter activity is best done with a good-sized group of hearty devotees who "pound" the suckers up- or down-stream—they move in a parallel line, banging on the ice—to a waiting line of "hookers" who wield long, spearlike poles. This can only be done in the dead of winter, which usually means January. That's because the river ice starts breaking up each year, quite predictably, in early February. The lower East Branch of the Delaware, which in places is very flat, is another stream

A mid-March morning on a Catskill lake.
Warm, misty, late-season days often make for the best fishing.

where sucker hooking has been popular. When Jimmy Petersen of the Silver Fox Tavern was still alive, he and his friends and guests would go hooking each year and then have a big fish fry at the tavern. Suckers taken from cold water can be very good eating.

Many a tough day on the ice is soothed by a few sensationally good-eating yellow perch, which happen to be active in winter. Bluegills and other sunfish, very nearly as good eating, are probably at least as widely distributed in Catskill lakes and ponds. Add crappies and scattered white perch and you have reasons enough to get up out of bed on an oh-so-cold mountain morning.

CHAPTER 7

Solitude on Lesser-Known Streams

E xploring away from the Catskill crowds led to one of the most memorable days I've ever had astream.

I didn't get to the Catskills until 3 P.M. on that June afternoon. I'd decided to fish the upper Rondout, so I took a left where Route 55A leaves Route 55 just east of Grahamsville. Then I drove toward Sundown and eventually found a place to park near the Little League ball field.

The small brook was at a normal height and gin clear. I wanted to see the inlet area where the stream joins Rondout Reservoir, so I began fishing downstream using a small spinner. Almost at once I picked up a pretty, 7-inch brook trout from behind a logjam. But that was the only fish that took and the inlet area was disappointing, so I trudged back up to the car.

After investigating the upper river and taking my notes, I drove back down the road to another Rondout tributary, one that had caught my eye earlier in the spring. It was Chestnut Creek, which flows from the west parallel to Route 55, crosses under Route 55 just east of 55A, then flows another few hundred yards before meeting Rondout Reservoir. Chestnut was flowing surprisingly full and fast. At the time, I didn't know why.

Because of the steep gradient, the water was so heavy below the Route

Wild trout nose into the froth of little pools like the one below this hidden waterfall. In the Catskills, there are still secret places for trout fishermen.

55 bridge that I could scarcely fish. So I made a scary wade across the stream to the south bank and walked downstream where the pitch of the streambed was less severe. I'd switched to a much larger gold spinning lure.

About 100 yards above the reservoir, and still in quite heavy water, the gold spinner stopped dead in its tracks. When the fish turned, it looked very silvery, and I thought maybe it was a rainbow. But while I could see the fish had some length, its fight was lackluster. Finally, when I got the fish within about 10 yards of shore I could see its markings, and I exclaimed out loud, "A brookie!" But then the fish came into focus and in the very next breath I exclaimed, "A laker!"

And it certainly was, 16 inches long with the tail deeply forked. I knew that lake trout had to be bigger than that in the reservoir, and I puzzled for a moment as to whether those regulations extended up into the tributaries. But the fish was skinny, and I wasn't inclined to keep it anyway. I let it slide back into Chestnut Creek, and then climbed the very steep bank back up to the road.

All of a sudden I got the inspiration that there was still time to hit the evening rise on the Beaver Kill. I laid the pedal down and quickly made it over the mountains to Livingston Manor and eventually the big river.

It was fly-rod time now, but I was disappointed when I got down to the bank to see few flies in the air. As the minutes ticked past the 7:30 mark, though, things picked up and some decent fish began working rhythmically.

It was one of those early-June complex hatches—tough. Finally, I duped a 13½-inch rainbow with a neutral-colored size 14 mayfly imitation, though by then it was nearly dark and I was nearly through. I made the last fly change of the night, to a highly visible Royal Wulff. No sooner had I done so than a little voice inside me told me to cut off the 5X tippet and get back to 4X. I did so. Then I stepped back to the edge of the darkening river.

I stalked the bank looking for one last fish, one good one. After several minutes I found what I was seeking in midcurrent.

When the fish took, it was dark enough that the two-toned dame's rocket on shore had already lost all its color. Oddly, I underestimated the size of the fish; I usually do the opposite with fish over 14 inches. But when it jumped I saw that it was a really good brownie.

The battle led me way downstream, and all the fly line was in the night air. I'm not sure at what point it happened, but a sudden chill came to me when I realized that if I landed this fish I would have taken a brookie, a brown, a rainbow, and a laker all in the same day. And all in streams! As the fish powered downstream, I seriously wondered if anyone had ever done that before in the Catskills. Now I wanted that fish badly.

Back at the car I laid the brown down and put a tape to it. It was 18 inches long and weighed 2 $\frac{3}{4}$ pounds. The next day I stuffed and baked it, and a friend and I offered it up in sacrifice to a unique Catskill afternoon.

The upper Rondout is a small creek. Let's take a brief look at it from where it joins the reservoir to its headwaters in the deep, exceptionally cold valley of the Peekamoose.

You might say that it ends at the Route 55A bridge, though if the lake is high the section just above the bridge will be inundated. The bridge itself is off limits to fishing, but just a few yards upstream you may enter, as the white sign says, for FISHING UNDER PERMIT ONLY. This is the watershed permit discussed in chapter 1. As soon as you get up above this immediate area of the reservoir, no permit is necessary.

This lower section is from that bridge up to East Mountain Road. The open-to-the-public city property extends about 0.6 mile above the bridge, and there are several nice pools here. One place to park would be by the Little League ball field. Park outside the gate in the grassy area, and be sure not to block the gate or you'll hold up the game. Walk down to the stream and you'll see that you can fish up- or downstream. Just upstream of the ball field there are some fields but also some posted signs. These seem to extend all the way up to East Mountain Road.

The next section is from East Mountain Road up to the next bridge, which crosses the river at Sundown. This, too, is mostly posted, with many old and new houses and some trailers located right on the river. At one point the stream carves a steep gorge, but here, too, are signs. You'll have to work to find access.

From Sundown up a bit there's been a spate of building and it's now too much backyard fishing for my liking, even though there probably is a bit of access. Finally, state land begins approximately 5.5 miles by road from Route 55, and most of the rest of the water from here upstream is on state land and thus open for fishing. This upper part of the river is very steep and scenic in places, and there are established campsites along Sundown Road (just sites, no facilities). Unfortunately, this area has suffered from overuse in recent years, and now you may camp only at designated and marked sites. Use of either of the two group sites requires a free permit.

You'll see a large opening on the left and a sign that reads SUNDOWN

WILD FOREST, PEEKAMOOSE VALLEY, LOWER FIELD PARKING, FOREST PRE-SERVE. Backpackers use this large parking area, but you can too. The stream is just a few dozen yards down below you. From the Region 3 office of the DEC (see page 211), request the brochure titled *Peekamoose Valley Wild Forest.* Also ask for the brochure or pamphlet on using forest preserve lands.

What you'll catch, by the way, is mostly small native brook trout. Still, a friend of mine who was deer hunting on the Peekamoose one November observed large browns migrating up the brook from the reservoir. Naturally, the season is over by then, but I've found that if a stream affords spawning for browns, they will sometimes randomly and inexplicably ascend that same stream during spring and summer, especially after some heavy rain. There are, by the way, a few surprisingly deep runs on the upper Rondout. If you're shunted upriver by posted signs, don't judge the stream too quickly from a few roadside glimpses.

Chestnut Creek is a small stream that wends its way through the Ulster County countryside, bisecting the village of Grahamsville. Approximately 300 yards upstream of Rondout Reservoir, water diverted from Neversink Reservoir periodically enters Chestnut and swells it greatly. This lower part of Chestnut, including the actual inlet area, is now off limits to fishermen. As for the rest of the stream, it gets low after midspring, but give it a try earlier in the season if you like small water. Chestnut Creek is stocked with several hundred brown trout annually.

Upper East Branch Delaware

The Delaware River system has made its way into several chapters, and that's not surprising: It's one of only three main drainage systems within the scope of this book, the others being the Hudson and the Susquehanna.

Of the rivers discussed in this chapter, the upper East Branch is where you might find the least solitude. But that's just because it's an ample stream, and a fine beat of water at that. These are the headwaters of the East Branch. The stream rises in the hilly country north of Roxbury, once the home of the great American naturalist and writer John Burroughs, and closely parallels Route 30 for some 20 miles before it's absorbed by the sprawling Pepacton Reservoir. The height of the reservoir at any given time determines where the river ends and the lake begins. The great Catskill flood of January 1996 really hit this area hard, but the stream is now starting to normalize.

Access is excellent. From the uppermost fishable water down to Margaretville, park along Route 30 or on the local road on the other side of the stream.

For a few miles up from the reservoir it is city property so access is guaranteed, but you do need a watershed permit to fish in this white-sign area. Here, below Margaretville, the river runs away from the road(s) in places, and is of a fair size and very interesting. It is actually quite a little hike in from Route 30 in spots. The water character is excellent: deep pools, swirling bends that deeply undermine tree roots, long runs, fast riffles—and still some debris and upturned trees lingering from the flood. There are both stocked and native browns here, in good numbers and sizes, and the banks are totally undeveloped thanks to the strip of city property. There is room here for all methods. I have found the hatches to be fine and diverse, though I haven't fished here enough to specifically chronicle them. One season two friends and I were fly-casting right below the gas station in Margaretville with a good hatch of gray foxes in the air. On another day, on that sexy water just above the first bridge above Pepacton, browns were rising freely to blue-winged olives.

Immediately above or upstream of Margaretville the river makes a big bend as it leaves the road, and where it again touches Route 30 there is an enormous pool that local residents enjoy all summer as a swimming hole. Not far above this is a golf course, but immediately north of the course is a nice rocky section where I've had some good fly-fishing. You're now in the vicinity of Kelly Corners.

From this point to the headwaters of the stream, access is where you find it, but a good starting point is the bridges. Go there and see what you find in the way of signs. A small but charming little community on the river is Halcottsville, where there's a bed & breakfast and a waterfalls. The East Branch is impounded at this point, and great blue herons plan their attack from pond's-edge loosestrife. On the day I visited recently, I saw two herons together, and on that same day I also saw two together on another stream. This great gawky bird was rare in these parts until about 15 years ago.

On recent forays I've found some nice water even above Halcottsville, including some fast, rocky sections a bit off the road. Posting is intermittent, but the effort expended at finding access may be worth it since I found plenty of trout up here. I might mention that I have caught a fair number of wild brook trout in the East Branch, even occasionally down by Pepacton. This stream seems to run fairly cold, and there may in fact be some brookies its entire length.

The nice midsized water above the golf course on the upper East Branch of the Delaware. Above this point, there is a mixture of slow, meadowlike water and rockier, faster sections.

Spawning browns also run up from Pepacton. Most of this will occur after the September 30 closing of the season, but some of these oversized browns are found in the stream from time to time during open season.

Little Beaver Kill

If you've fished the Beaver Kill or otherwise frequented the Roscoe area, you've no doubt stopped at one time or another at the snack stand at Parksville. Perhaps you've even mused at the little brook that flows under the Quickway right next to the store. This is the Little Beaver Kill, and it's not only a very charming small stream, it's a very ignored one. Below its halfway point, it's more a midsized than a small stream. Anglers have 2.9 bank miles of public easements to work with, and many private sections are not posted.

It emanates from North Pond roughly 5 miles northeast of Route 17, then turns and flows north-northwest for another 6 miles from the Parksville traffic light to the stream's confluence with the Willowemoc in Livingston Manor. It's clearly visible from the Quickway for part of the way.

The Little Beaver Kill actually feeds the Willowemoc right inside the village of Livingston Manor. You must have a good local road map to be able to follow it to where it emerges at the Quickway.

Just about 0.75 mile outside of the Manor, you come to a Y as you're heading southeast on a local road. If you stay right, you almost immediately come to an angler's parking lot that denotes a state easement. The stream is right behind the lot, and this water both up and down is extremely nice.

Go back to the Y and this time take the left fork. You'll cross the Little Beaver Kill in short order, and immediately past it make a left. This quiet, country road will more or less parallel the stream all the way to Route 17, and you'll find some open water and plenty of trout in the 14- to 16-inch class, if not better. The water character is superb.

You will, as I said, emerge at Route 17, the Quickway, and you should make a right onto it. For the next 2 miles or so, the right shoulder of the Quickway is your best and only access to the stream; simply park where you can and walk on down. After those 2 miles, you'll come to Fox Mountain Road. (Just beyond this on the opposite side of the Quickway are a gas station and a diner.) Make a right onto Fox Mountain Road and after only 150 yards you'll see a small stream on your right, Benton Hollow Brook. Park just before the bridge on the right side where, at present, there are no signs. Follow the little feeder down a few yards to reach an extremely deep pool where Benton Hollow meets the Little Beaver Kill. Not only is this a killer pool, easily capable of handling a 20-inch trout, but from here you can fish the Little Beaver Kill upstream or down.

To see more of this stream, go back up Fox Mountain Road to the Quickway and make a right onto it, so that once again you are heading east. From here to the traffic light at Parksville, the Little Beaver Kill will be on your right. At present, there are some abandoned businesses and grassy parking lots on the right shoulder, and you can park in one of these and walk down to the stream. Within this section is a locally well-known small waterfall, which is part of a series of rapids caused by a sudden drop in the stream's elevation. As of recently, you could park on the shoulder of the Quickway right by the falls and fish upstream or down as you wish. When Route 17 becomes Interstate 86, these access points along the Little Beaver Kill may vanish.

Above Parksville the Little Beaver Kill is quite small, and in summer its flows are paltry. With a good spring freshet, though, there is viable water above Parksville. Indeed, between the light at Route 17 and the first bridge upstream, there is some lovely small water and, as of recently, unposted bank property. Admittedly, above that first bridge the stream diminishes to the size of a small mountain brook trout stream.

The Little Beaver Kill is stocked with about 2,000 yearling browns and 200 two-year-old browns each season. I've also taken a few very chunky native brook trout from this stream. I'd be willing to bet that there are a fair number of these. With rainbow trout penetrating ever higher into the Delaware River system, I also wouldn't be surprised to start catching that species here.

I have no hard data on hatches, but stomach autopsies on several trout revealed the following: many small, greenish caddis worms, including those with pebble cases; very small mayfly nymphs; mostly immature but also a few mature stonefly nymphs; and some miscellaneous bugs like spiders, mites, and even a few ticks!

Callicoon Creek

Callicoon Creek is a true "local stream." I'm willing to bet that 90 percent of the pressure it gets is from local residents, and even that pressure is not excessive. I'll first discuss what is often called the East Branch of Callicoon Creek, even though it's really the main stem of the river.

Callicoon is a stream that wears several different faces. Sometimes you see the face of a classic meadow stream, with slow, deep, and still pools. Trout cruise the surface on a torpid summer day and nonselectively pick off whatever bugs there be. At times it's all riffles, with too little slope, and the sun beating down; deeper water must be sought, or higher-water periods awaited, on these sections. In places it's a true son of the mountains, its heavily shaded waters tumbling cataract-style through miniature gorges. This countenance is a little too nice; its owners covet it, and there are posted signs in obnoxious abundance.

Let's call the upper section that water between the pleasant Catskill communities of Youngsville and Jeffersonville, along Route 52. At the first bridge over the stream below Youngsville, Dewitt Flats Road, it is already a good-sized brook, at least in spring. Here I saw sculpins in the shallows and two 10-inch trout pacing nervously back and forth. There were hundreds of caddis stick larvae in the rocks, and the deep water was inviting. I saw no posted signs recently, so you may be able to park at this bridge and fish up or down—just don't tell them I said so.

From that bridge down to Briscoe Road, the stream is at times far off the road. There are some fields that not along ago were farms, and the posting is spotty. Access can be tried for off Route 52 or off the road that parallels the stream on the opposite side. In general, this upstream water is deeper than the Callicoon Creek most people know from Hortonville down to the big Delaware.

Immediately below Briscoe Road the stream is starting to back up as it becomes impounded into Lake Jefferson. You'll want to skip downstream to below this lake and the considerable activity of "Jeff."

Just south of the main part of Jeffersonville there are a few pull-offs on the left side that might afford some access. At one point the banks are very steep, and the stream fairly fast. Below this, the river runs tight to Route 52 and there is some access here, too. Before heading downstream to the bigger water you can pause at the Stone Arch Bridge County Park, a well-known and restful Sullivan County landmark, and look over your map or have lunch. This, by the way, is where Route 52 that you've been following turns off to Fosterdale. You don't make that left—you stay straight.

You are now on Route 52A and a very short way below the junction you'll see a sign that marks a public easement. A sign says ANGLERS PARK HERE. I did so, and walked the 25-yard cleared path down to the stream. What I found was a gorgeous pool, a startled deer wading in the shallows, and joe-pye weed over my head.

Still heading downstream you'll see the Diehl farm on your right, where you can buy some honey or maple syrup. There are a couple more angler access points on the left near the farm. One especially nice pool lies beneath a small condemned bridge. It seems as if all the bridge pools on Callicoon Creek are very deep. Eventually you'll come to a bridge and another turn to Fosterdale. Again, don't make this turn; stay straight. But before you do, you can park at this bridge and fish a bit up- or downstream.

You will now be on Route 17B the rest of the way down to Callicoon, but often the brook isn't visible from the road. Unfortunately, here is where the posted signs that have so far been spotty begin in earnest. The river now cuts an increasingly deep notch and only near the bottom end of this notch, where the stream comes very close to the road, may there be a little bit of open water. This would be worth checking into.

From Eschenberg's chain saw place down to Hortonville posting is intermittent, but as of recently there was some access with parking on the shoulder of Route 17B. There is some very beautiful water here, and while it's not terribly deep, in spring it should be just fine.

From the little hamlet of Hortonville down to Callicoon is about 2 miles and there are some state easements here. This is for the most part a rocky, riffly section but not a very deep one, and part of this beat is highly exposed to the sun. I especially like the part of this section about 300 yards upstream from the Callicoon's junction with the main stem Delaware. There is easement parking and good access via local roads in the community of Callicoon.

There are wild rainbows in the lower Callicoon, and spawners from the main stem Delaware probably ascend in early spring. There are also some wild brookies and browns, and, in addition, the state stocks Callicoon with a large number of brown trout.

In spring you will usually find good water flows and pleasant fishing conditions. From late spring onward, much of the stream will look low and unwelcoming. Wait for a good rain.

One of the experts who looked at this chapter was a bit aghast that I had not mentioned the North Branch of Callicoon Creek. Although it's a fairly small stream, it maintains a good population of wild browns and rainbows, with the rainbows thought to be more numerous. In this thin water, trout seek out the deeper holes to ride out any dry weather. Despite the occurrence of wild fish, the DEC stocks a large number of browns in the North Branch.

Anglers can thank DEC personnel for having sought and obtained public fishing easements to the North Branch of Callicoon Creek. There are about 9 bank miles of easements, and that's how long the stream is, so that you can fish most of the stream from one side or the other. There are several anglers' parking lots, and they are easy to spot. If you're coming up from the village of Callicoon, simply make a left at Hortonville and the North Branch will be on your right side all the way up to its headwaters. On this note, I should mention that one of the downsides of fishing this heavily shaded stream is that the road runs so closely to it.

Mongaup River

It's easy to tell that the Mongaup was once an exquisitely beautiful river, because vestiges of that beauty remain today. Regrettably, no sizable Catskill river has been so impacted by man. When I say "impacted" I really mean "impounded," because there are five reservoirs on the Mongaup system, as well as numerous ponds and lakes. There are also bungalow colonies, hydroelectric generating stations, high tension lines, houses and other dwellings,

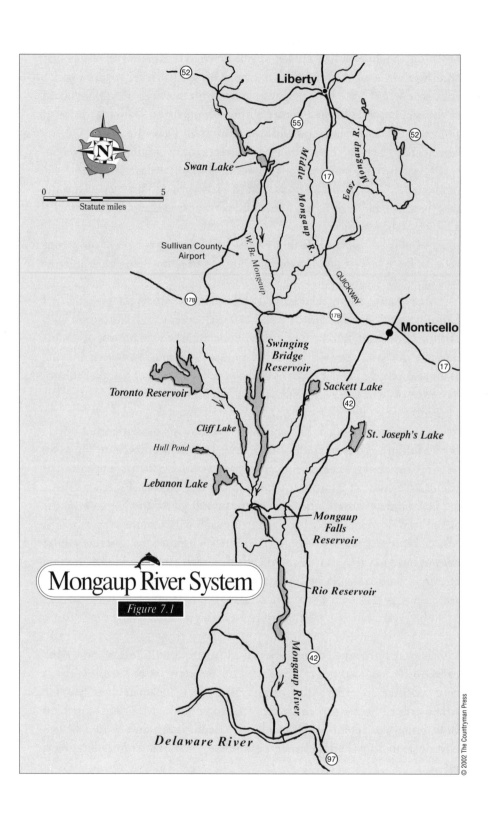

Liberty

52

55

Swan Lake

Middle Mongaup R.

East Mongaup R.

52

17

0   5
Statute miles

Sullivan County Airport

W. Br. Mongaup

17B

QUICKWAY

17B

Monticello

17

Swinging Bridge Reservoir

Toronto Reservoir

Sackett Lake

42

Cliff Lake

St. Joseph's Lake

Hull Pond

Lebanon Lake

Mongaup Falls Reservoir

Mongaup River System

Figure 7.1

Rio Reservoir

Mongaup River

42

Delaware River

97

© 2002 The Countryman Press

restaurants built literally over the river, old quarries and gravel pits, campgrounds and marinas, bridges and roads, and roads and more roads.

At present there are no state easements on the Mongaup above Swinging Bridge Reservoir. Posting is relatively heavy, but there are still open sections. These must be hunted out. On the lower Mongaup, below Rio Reservoir (see figure 7.1), there is indeed public fishing—several miles' worth, as we'll discuss.

Three little fingers of water coalesce in the Liberty area and eventually join together to form the mother river. The Middle Mongaup River, as it's called, emanates from several little ponds northeast of Liberty and about a mile west of Neversink Reservoir. It then makes its way through the city of Liberty where, besides the ignominy of the city and the Quickway having been built right on top of it, its banks have been recently stripped for God only knows what purpose. It's still a very small brook at Liberty.

Almost immediately downstream of Liberty, though, it begins to take on the character and look of a true trout stream, and I've taken a few nice fish practically within sight of the golden arches in town. From this southern fringe of Liberty down to about Bushville, posting is fairly intense. Just south of Bushville it's joined by the East Branch Mongaup, an interesting and somewhat secluded, slow, and meandering meadow brook that comes in from the northeast. It would be worth exploring this stream, and to help you do so, get the Monticello and Liberty East topographical quadrangles. There is no one large road paralleling the Mongaup, as with most other major Catskill rivers. Maps, therefore, are essential. By the way, the East Branch upstream of Route 17 is stocked with trout, about 1,200 browns a year.

After the East Branch enters, our stream is now properly called the Mongaup River. Below this junction, the Mongaup traverses some very pretty farm country, land that has somewhat (for now) been spared the ever-expanding development in Sullivan County. Once again, access points must be sleuthed out. Because parking and access are so tricky on the entire upper Mongaup above Swinging Bridge, I recommend that you make an exploratory trip.

The West Branch of the Mongaup is also a very nice little stream, which, like other little brooks in the area, now has beavers working it. It emanates from the area of Swan Lake, southwest of Liberty, and flows through some lightly settled countryside where there still are a few active farms. Access is here and there. In terms of size, this branch starts to look nice about where it passes under Fraser Road. From this road south for a mile or two, the West Branch flows just to the east of Creamery Road. The Sullivan County Airport is just to the west of this. This nice part of the river is well off the road in

A glimpse of the lower Mongaup where it joins the Main Stem Delaware.
Because of a power generating station at Rio Reservoir dam,
water levels fluctuate markedly in this home stretch of the Mongaup.

places, but you'll have to be willing to use your topo maps and find little spots where there are no posted signs. Close friends who have fished this section near the airport have reported some good action on browns. The West Branch is stocked with a few hundred trout, principally in its lower end near the junction with the main stem.

About 0.75 mile north or upstream of Route 17B, the West Branch joins the main stem. Near this junction you'll find wild browns of at least 15 to 16 inches. There is some very nice water here, both in the lower West Branch and in the main stem just upstream of the West Branch junction. Here a number of apparently abandoned gravel pits hug the river. Follow the dirt roads that go down into these old quarries and you will find places to fish both the main stem and the lower West Branch. While doing so this past summer, I saw wild turkeys running around the premises.

Now we are down to Route 17B. This should be where the best trout water actually starts but, unfortunately, only a few hundred yards below 17B begins a string of three reservoirs that were formed upon the Mongaup. From north to south, and as shown on figure 7.1, they are Swinging Bridge, Mongaup Falls, and Rio.

The very short segments of river between these three reservoirs have suffered from anoxia or oxygen starvation, and, in addition, sections of them are now closed to angling because of the ongoing effort to protect the growing eagle population.

The best opportunity on the entire Mongaup is below Rio Reservoir, for here there are about 3.5 miles of river with guaranteed access for fishermen. One place to park is right by the Rio dam, as discussed in chapter 6. Another established parking lot is a short way south of the Rio dam. Cross the dam from east to west and bear left onto a local road. About 1.7 miles from the dam you'll see a turn to the left. Make that left and then another immediate left. You'll see a sign that says WHITE WATER ACCESS FACILITY—PUBLIC ACCESS—8 A.M. TO SUNSET—4/15 TO 8/31. Follow the dirt road down to an open gate. Go through the gate and bear right. You'll soon come to the stream, just below the power generating station. Kayakers use this put-in point, but fishing is allowed too. By the way, don't be deterred by any signs spuriously erected by local residents to keep people out. You have a right to be here.

You can also park by Route 97 right near the main Delaware and fish upstream. The signs on the trees clearly mark this as public fishing water. There is a woods road heading upstream from Route 97 on the south side of the river that provides a very convenient means of access.

Because of a lack of roads near the stream, the farther down from Rio or farther up from Route 97 you go, the less likely you are to see any other fishermen.

This lower stretch of the Mongaup is very steep, rocky, and in places almost awesome in beauty. It may not qualify for the term *gorge*, but the banks are almost vertical in places. Despite the fairly heavy nutrient enrichment passed down from the valley above, the cold releases from Rio greatly help the trout fishing.

Actually, the severe water-level fluctuations caused by the power generating facility below the Rio dam may hurt the fishing more than the fish. When the river is up, the fishing is often quite good. When it's down, it is often very poor. But there is always enough water coming down that the trout can survive. Very shady conditions must help to keep the reduced flows cool in midsummer.

These are all wild trout. Browns predominate, and while biologists tell me that the population density is not great, the average size of the fish is very good, with many 13- to 15-inch fish present. I have also caught brook trout up to 12 or 13 inches, among the larger brookies I've caught in the Catskills.

A word of warning—actually two words. First, water levels can rise quickly. Keep an eye out for this. Especially heavy recreational releases are made for kayakers several times a year. The dates of these are sometimes posted at the aforementioned parking spot 1.7 miles below the Rio dam. Second, wading here can be conservatively described as excruciatingly torturous. It's worse down near Route 97. This is a dangerous situation, so bad in places that your best strategy would be not to wade at all—just cast from shore where you can. Spin-fishermen have an advantage, since fly-casters really need to wade to get away from snarling overhead foliage.

Finally, you should know that this entire lower end of the Mongaup below Rio has special regulations: Only artificial lures may be used, and the limit is three trout per day 12 inches or larger. The season here is statewide, or April 1 through October 15.

Catskill Creek

Although it lies out of the mainstream of Catskill trout fishing, this is a major trout stream in both size and length. Traversing three counties—Schoharie, Albany, and Greene—it flows, carves, tumbles, and cascades for nearly 38 miles before joining the Hudson River at Catskill.

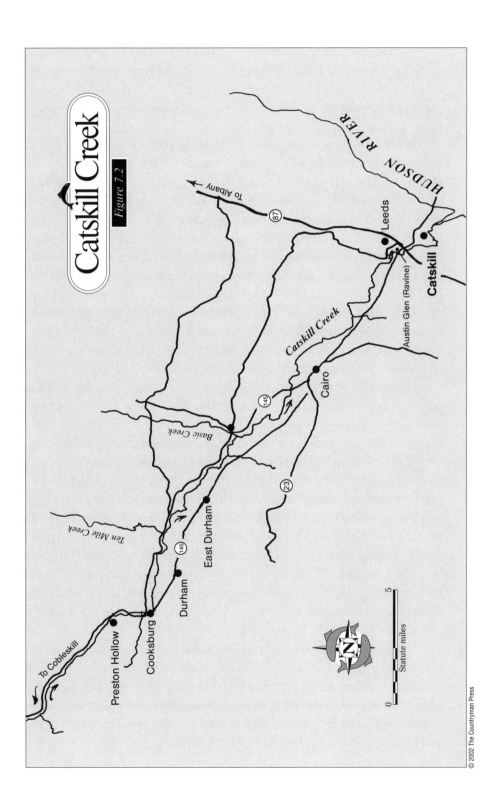

Catskill Creek

Figure 7.2

Statute miles

© 2002 The Countryman Press

The Catskill Mountains' namesake river is truly beautiful where the road is not right on top of it. It's characterized by often precipitous drops in gradient, creating magnificent cataracts and waterfalls. Although the river does get very low in summer, these deep pools must provide some measure of refuge for the trout.

Catskill Creek has a possibly declining population of wild, self-sustaining rainbows. In the upper reaches, 'bows dominate the picture and are abundant. Here in the Catskill Creek headwaters an 8- or 9-inch rainbow is a good fish, and there are many that will just tape out at 7 inches. As you move downstream, you may encounter rainbows that are somewhat larger, but not by a whole lot. Although the transition zone between cold-water species (trout) and warm-water species will vary depending on weather conditions, the village of Freehold is often cited as the dividing line. Below Freehold it's principally a warm-water fishery, and when you get down to Leeds the smallmouth fishing is quite good. There are also some chain pickerel and panfish. Near Freehold, brown trout will outnumber the rainbows by a considerable margin. Only browns are stocked; they're put in from about a mile downstream of Freehold up to the Greene County line.

The access picture at Catskill Creek is excellent. There are about 17 bank miles of state easements, and much of the private water has not yet been closed off with heavy posting.

Other Waters of the Northeastern Catskills

Although atmospheric pollution has dulled the view over time, one of the greatest prospects in all of New York State must surely be from the site of the Old Catskill Mountain House hotel. It is said that you can see 50 miles of the Hudson River from this precipice, and what glorious days the fair ladies and fine-dressed men of the Gilded Age must have spent at this site and in that quieter time. While we can argue endlessly about where the Catskills end at the other three points on the compass, here in the east there can be no doubt.

Through the precipitous mountain canyons that terminate at this almost sheer eastern escarpment flow some of the most inscrutable trout streams in the Catskills. Most are tiny and some are intermittent, but at least one offers adequate flows all year, and it just begs for exploration. I'm that type, and the fact that Kaaterskill Creek has still largely escaped my glare speaks to the sheer difficulty of getting down to it.

Or at least, getting down to the part that interests me. It begins in tame enough fashion just northeast of the village of Haines Falls, and crosses under Route 23A just about at that village. It isn't long, though, before it drops into an incredible Catskill "clove" or steep valley. I'm sure hikers have been down into this great rift valley, but no anglers I know have gone there and come back to tell about it. Wild brook trout or rainbow trout in the greeny deeps of dazzling plunge pools? I don't know, but one day I will find the way down in. By the topographical maps I have, it appears that part of the steepest and most difficult section is part state land and part private. I see only three possible means of entry: from the vicinity of Haines Falls, from a parking area near where the outlet of South Lake crosses under Route 23 (it eventually feeds into the Kaaterskill), and from the point nearer Palenville at which the stream emerges from the abyss and crosses under Route 23A from south to north. You could, of course, try the stream around Haines Falls and up- or downstream a way, but I am unsure about public access to this more available part of the river.

Far less vertical but still very intriguing and certainly more accessible is the East Kill, an important midsized stream that feeds Schoharie Creek at Jewett Center. It rises just a few short miles from the eastern escarpment, and flows west and then south to add much-needed water to the mother river. The East Kill's 13 miles lie smack in the center of Greene County.

Rich with good holding lies and varied water, the East Kill has about 1.1 bank miles of public easement, and more than 5 miles of it are stocked. It does not have as much of the easily eroded clay as does its sister stream, the West Kill, and it did not suffer the extreme damage wreaked on the West Kill in the January flood of 1996.

The easement water is just upstream of Jewett Center, and this happens to also be very nice water. In summer local residents swim here, which tells you that the East Kill has some very deep pools. Above this stretch the creek is often far away from the road, and while there certainly is much posted property, the tenacious explorer will find some access. County Routes 17 and 23C, and State Route 296 provide your means of entry to this watershed. While I've fished it but little, I just have a hunch about it.

The Batavia Kill flows essentially west from its headwaters in the Blackhead Mountains east of Maplecrest to its confluence with Schoharie Creek a mile upstream of Prattsville (see figure 3.2). It's a very substantial creek, nearly 20 miles long, and while there are only a few miles of public fishing water, posting at present is only moderate. On a recent summertime foray I found extreme weediness in the upper section, and this no doubt stems from the fact that there is much active agriculture in the valley. Fishing pressure is light, and while everyone I spoke with said there are trout here, no one was writing any poems about the river. Only brown trout are stocked—6,000 in the most recent year—and they are planted at intervals from Maplecrest all the way down to Schoharie Creek.

Catskill Creek has many trout-holding tributaries, among them Basic Creek, which is stocked with about 1,600 trout, and Tenmile Creek, which is not listed in stocking reports. Both of these originate in Albany County and flow north to south. While almost no one considers Albany County part of the Catskills, it is quite hilly and it does have some good trout streams.

A tributary that enters Catskill Creek from the south and also isn't stocked is the Shingle Kill. While I haven't fished it, contacts up that way tell me that it holds some big trout.

Seeking Public Fishing Water

Where can I find access to some of the good trout water today? In the Catskills, as elsewhere in populous New York, that sticky question supersedes such secondary concerns as what fly to use or what weight line to deploy. Happily, there is a great deal of public water in the Catskills. You just have to know what to look for, and where.

With great farsightedness, the New York State Department of Environmental Conservation (DEC) began acquiring streambank easements as far back as the mid-1930s. This innovative and far-reaching program now allows access to hundreds of miles of prime trout water across the state that almost certainly would have otherwise been closed off to the public. These easements are across private land, which means that fishermen must restrict their activities to the stream and its bank or banks. A good example is the Beaver Kill. Almost the entire lower Beaver Kill from Roscoe to East Branch is open to fishermen via state-secured easements. As on many other streams with easements, there are well-marked parking areas for anglers, and anglers should use these when possible—their purpose is, in part, to encourage anglers to use access points that will be least disturbing to landowners.

Another good-as-gold situation is water that bisects state lands. Within the boundaries of the Catskill Park, state land is termed forest preserve, land that our state constitution protects as "forever wild." There are about 750,000 acres of forest preserve lands in the Catskills, and through them flow such

With tailwaters and big trout on their minds, most of today's anglers unforgiveably fail to take a look at some of the midsized and small waters farther up in the mountains. The reward for a little bit of independent thinking can be miles of stream to yourself.

streams as the upper East Branch of the Neversink, discussed in chapter 3, and upper Rondout Creek, covered in this chapter. You can pitch a tent and camp for free on state lands, although for the most part you can't camp closer than 150 feet from water.

Just on the fringes of the forest preserve, but still very much in the Catskills, are parcels of land termed multiple use areas. These lands are open to hiking, hunting, and sometimes other forms of outdoor recreation, and where fishing exists it's usually permitted. An example is Crystal Lake in Sullivan County, where you can try for wild brook trout.

In some instances, good water bisects a state campground, and especially if you like to camp this is a possibility you should investigate. One example would be the Beaver Kill Campground on the upper part of that river. Another would be Woodland Valley Campground on Woodland Valley Creek near Phoenicia. See the chart in the chapter 8 essay.

There's often public fishing in special areas owned or managed by the state. Two categories that quickly come to mind are state parks and wildlife management areas (WMAs). With parks, a good example would be Lake Superior State Park, which offers bass and panfish and is discussed in chapter 6.

WMAs are more apt to be thought of for hunting, but where a lake or stream exists on a WMA it is usually open to angling. Just outside the Catskills but discussed in this book is Sullivan County's Bashakill State Wildlife Management Area; it offers some very good warm-water fishing. Another example is the Mongaup Valley Wildlife Management Area, discussed fully in this book. Still another is Delaware County's Bear Spring Mountain, mentioned in chapter 8.

A type of private land where public fishing may sometimes be allowed is a state cooperative area or "co-op." On these private lands, sometimes groups of adjacent farms, the state has secured hunting rights. Sometimes fishing is also allowed, as in the Ten Mile River, which falls within the Ten Mile River Cooperative Area in southern Sullivan County. I've recently been informed that there is a permit system here.

Yet more public fishing water can at times be found within a state unique area. This is a relatively new classification for state land, and each unique area has its own "unique" set of governing rules and regulations. A fine example in the Catskills region is the Neversink Gorge, where anglers can try for wild trout amid a truly wild setting. This fishing is discussed in chapter 3.

CHAPTER 8

The Peaceful Face of the Northern Catskills

There is a peaceful place in the Catskill Mountains, a land of undulating hills and dairy cows, schoolboy farm streams, and gentle little villages. Here, far from the glitz of big resorts and the clamor of Monticello Raceway, you can still find a stream to call your own. It is the undiscovered Catskills, a crescent of land extending across the northern two-thirds of Delaware County and into Schoharie County (figures 8.1 and 8.3). The actual fishing is not on a par with the Delaware River below the dams, but there are some moderately productive waters, and the scenery—ah, the scenery. You may look far and wide across this good earth and not find lovelier countryside.

Upper West Branch Delaware River

This river remains one of the great unknowns of Catskill trout fishing. Rising just northeast of Stamford, this, the farthest reach of the Delaware River, tracks roughly southwest as it parallels Route 10 almost its entire course. From its headwaters near South Jefferson in Schoharie County to its terminus at Cannonsville Reservoir is a remarkable 45 miles.

I think it is fair to call this a farm stream. Although there are some riffly sections, there are many more medium to slow sections, and farmland does hug the river for much of the way. The gradient is a gradual 10.8 feet per mile.

Brown trout predominate here. There are a few brook trout, all wild, but not many. Only browns are stocked, about 15,000 in a recent year. Holdover is reasonably good, though growth rates are not as good as in the water below Cannonsville Dam. For example, a 12-inch brown in the upper West Branch is typically three years old. Below the dam a trout that length will be only two years old. Water temperature is the key factor (see chapter 9).

About 30 percent of the browns in the upper West Branch are wild. There is virtually no reproduction in the main West Branch, but most of the tributaries in this area support wild, self-sustaining trout. What wild browns are found in the main river have come down from the tributaries. In spring, in fact, I recommend that you try some of these West Branch feeders. Browns will usually be most prevalent in the lower ends of the tributaries, while the wild brookies may be concentrated farther upstream. This is not a hard-and-fast rule, though. In some northern Catskill streams, brookies will predominate while in other places browns will. From these cold mountain rills, all trout will be firm and good tasting. Also, some larger browns from the main river that ascend a tributary in fall to spawn may linger into spring, to provide an unexpected thrill for an early-season angler.

Fishing pressure is generally light, while at the same time catch rates are quite good. Fly-fishing can be practiced anywhere, and while it may be most enjoyable in the larger water below Delhi, even upstream the brook is open enough to allow fly-casting. Access is excellent. Posting by private landowners is not heavy, and in general the attitude toward anglers is friendly. There are also many miles of public easements for fishermen. Most of these easements are between the junction of Routes 26 and 10 at Hamden, and Stamford. A high percentage of the water between Delhi and Stamford is public easement water. About half a dozen anglers' parking lots have been established by the DEC and these, plus streambank signs, help mark the easement stretches. All these parking lots are along Route 10, and all are easy to locate. Just park in the lot and walk down to fish. There is also generally good access at the bridges, and since anglers tend to stay near them, a walk up- or downstream will often reward you with long stretches of stream to yourself.

Let's take a closer look, starting at Cannonsville Reservoir and working upstream.

The first section is from the reservoir to Walton. The length of this sec-

Northern Delaware County

Figure 8.1

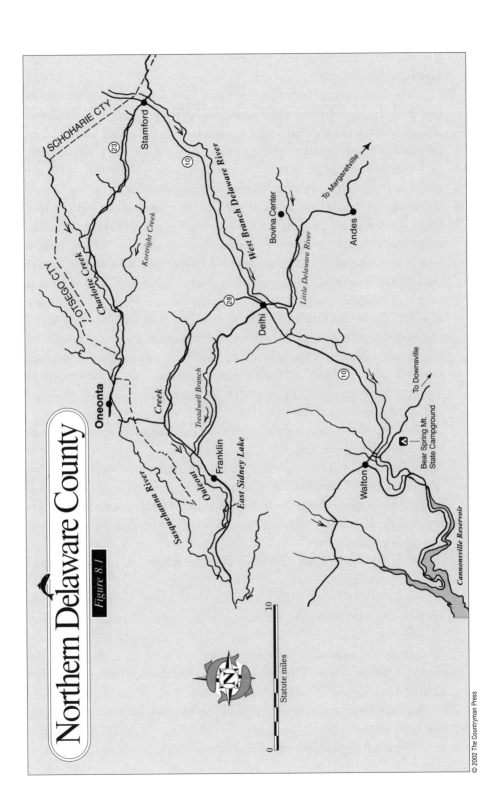

Statute miles

tion can vary from about 5 to 8 miles depending on the height of the reservoir at any given time.

One day in spring I was driving north on Route 10. The reservoir was extremely high, and there were some flooded fields along the section that would normally have been river. I saw some large fish breaking water, so I excitedly clambered down with fishing rod in hand. As I feared, they were large carp rolling on the surface. Carp are plentiful in Cannonsville, and if this species strikes your fancy, look for this particular situation in spring.

From the first bridge below Walton downstream a short way is a nice, rocky, shady section. In truth, not too much of the river has this nice, mountain-stream look. I encountered excellent hatches of Hendricksons here, as well as little blue quills, and the trout were cooperative. The wading is often challenging, because of the slippery rocks—wear appropriate wading gear. To fish this stretch, simply park by the bridge and walk down. If the reservoir is at full pool, you won't walk far. I recently caught small wild browns here.

Above that bridge, the West Branch flattens out into pasturelands. It's considerably off the main road here, and in places is best accessed by the farm road that parallels Route 10. Where the stream does cut off away from the main road, it is usually through a farm. Requesting permission to fish from the farmers along the way should draw favorable results, although from a practical standpoint, finding the farmer at the moment you want to fish may not be easy.

Approximately 1 mile upstream of the aforementioned bridge, the river is again rocky and fast as it hugs a steep bank on its northwest side. You can park in any of the few little pull-offs on Route 10 and clamber on down to the stream. This riffly section is very inviting, and locals here tell of some good trout in this section.

Above this and on up to Walton the river really opens up as it courses through pasturelands.

Section 2 of the upper West Branch is from Walton to Delhi. Just above Walton I saw, on that same day, a great Hendrickson hatch, and dimples from bank to bank. I parked on Route 10 just upstream of Walton—again, no posting—and stumbled right into a problem I'd often heard about here: chubs. But they took my fly, tussled a little, and I cursed them not. But I didn't catch any trout in this fairly flat section.

From Walton to Delhi the banks of the river are intensely farmed, yet this is some of the nicest water. Heading north on Route 10, make a right onto County Route 26 just before the Octagon Farm Market, where there is also a bed & breakfast. You will almost immediately come to the river; park on either side and take a look off the bridge. You are as likely to see a 10-pound carp as a 12-inch trout, but there is some truly pleasant water upstream toward Hamden and also downstream a ways, and much of this is public easement. I've seen canoes put in at this bridge, although it's not the most convenient location to do so. While I haven't canoed this river, it would seem to be a great way to get at the many off-the-road pools.

Section 3 of the upper West Branch is from Delhi to Stamford, a long 18 miles. Here it's a most charming meadow stream that reminds me of the Columbia County brooks I fished as a boy. If you dote on exploring small water, and like the smell of cow manure as well as having literally miles of trout stream almost to yourself, you may have found your soul mate.

While trout are resident here, suckers and even a few unseemly bullheads own timeshares. In addition, parts of the stream are highly exposed to the sun. I suggest that you fish this section in early or midspring, or later in the season when a good rain has perked up the river.

Little Delaware

I recently drove along this entire river, and my earlier impression that it's mostly posted was only confirmed. This is regrettable, because it's a beautiful small to midsized stream, with much more fast water than the upper West Branch, which it joins at Delhi. Angling pressure is probably extremely light.

There are two short state easements west of Glen Bernie Road, but the locations of these are by no means apparent from Route 28. About 0.75 mile from Route 10 is a pull-off that brings you down to a kiosk and self-guiding nature trail. This is probably the westernmost of those two easements.

It was June 8. The meadow was stunning with dame's rocket, and there were a few green drakes over the water, as well as a few *Isonychia* nymph cases on the river rocks. No fish were to be seen on this bright sunny day, but officials say "there are lots of trout." It's beautiful dry-fly water here, but it's so slippery I don't know how you'd wade it for long. Because of the slippery rocks, and the lack of established paths streamside, use the nature trail to your advantage.

Local Route 6 will bring you to the hamlets of Bovina Center and Bovina, two charming and truly off-the-beaten-path Catskill communities. Alas, the posting on the river continues. It's not until you reach the true headwaters of the Little Delaware that the public easements resume, but here it's very tiny water.

An excellent base of operations for fishing these northern Catskill waters would be the Bear Spring Mountain State Campground, located just off Route 206 between Downsville and Walton. The spare facilities—no flush toilets or showers, and no hook-ups—seem to draw a quiet, respectful clientele. A nice bonus is the several trout ponds on the Bear Spring property, including Launt Pond right at the campground. It's stocked with brookies and rainbows, and one regular visitor told me he once caught an 18-inch rainbow here. In early June I encountered mayfly spinner flights and cooperative but selective fish. *Hint:* Rent the rowboat and head down to the quieter end of the lake for the evening hatch.

Oquaga Creek

Let's now shift geographically to the extreme northwest corner of the Catskills, to pretty little Oquaga Creek. While this book does not otherwise cover areas west of Delaware County, I am including Oquaga (located mostly in Broome County) because it is a significant part of the Delaware drainage.

In 1966 a 3-mile segment of this interesting little farm stream was made no-kill, making it one of the earliest New York State streams to be so designated. On this no-kill beat, artificial lures only are permitted, all fish must be released, and the season is year-round. On the rest of the stream the season runs from April 1 through October 15. For the location of Oquaga Creek, see figure 9.2 in chapter 9.

From its confluence with the West Branch Delaware at Deposit upstream to the Quickway bridge at McClure—the no-kill falls within this stretch—Oquaga sports adequate flows and pretty, varied water. You get a few glimpses of it as you traverse Route 17, but some of it is out of view. There are a few houses and farms, and floodplain cornfields run right up to the bank in many places.

There are 4.19 miles of state easements on Oquaga, much of this on the lower end. Other than that, you can use the train tracks that parallel the river to gain access to lightly fished sections. There is also adequate space on the shoulder of old Route 17, if you plan to fish downstream of McClure.

Upstream of the Route 17 bridge at McClure, Oquaga Creek reaches quite a few miles to its headwaters in Broome State Forest. Easements occur intermittently between McClure and Sanford. Above Sanford, however, the

Oquaga Creek is an important tributary to the Delaware's West Branch, but it's a nice midsized stream in its own right. The water is varied, and in its upper half, wild brook trout mingle with some very nice-sized browns.

stream is quite small. Both above and below this hamlet, the angling pressure is light and comes almost completely from local people, many of whom fish bait with rods propped up on sticks.

Oquaga Creek is annually stocked with about 4,500 brown trout. Large trout from the West Branch must surely use Oquaga for spawning, and may ascend at least the lower end of this tributary during periods of heavy rain.

East Sidney Lake

While exploring northern Delaware County one early-summer day, I came upon East Sidney Lake (see figure 8.1). This 210-acre impoundment was formed on Ouleout Creek just a few miles above that stream's confluence with the Susquehanna, and is part of flood-control efforts on the Susquehanna drainage. It's owned by the Army Corps of Engineers, but managed by the town of Sidney. In the lake-poor northern Catskills, it offers a combination of amenities that will appeal to many.

First, bass boats are permitted, and there are no restrictions on horsepower. Second, camping is allowed here, so if you like to combine fishing, boating, and camping, this place may strike your fancy. All general New York

COUNTY	NAME OF LAKE OR POND	PRINCIPAL GAMEFISH

Figure 8.2. *A sample of lakes and ponds outside the Lake District*

COUNTY	NAME OF LAKE OR POND	PRINCIPAL GAMEFISH
DELAWARE	LAUNT POND	ST, RT
DELAWARE	BIG POND	RT, LMB, SMB, CP, BT
DELAWARE	MUD POND	BT, RT
DELAWARE	TROUT POND	ST
GREENE	COLGATE LAKE	BT
GREENE	NORTH & SOUTH LAKE	PANFISH, SOME BASS
GREENE	GREEN'S LAKE	BT, RT, LMB, CP, KOK
GREENE	NEW COXSACKIE RES.*	LMB
GREENE	CATSKILL RES.*	LMB, CP
GREENE	HOLLISTER LAKE*	LMB
ULSTER	ALDER LAKE	ST
ULSTER	CHODIKEE LAKE	LMB, CP
ULSTER	ECHO LAKE	ST
ULSTER	FOURTH BINNEWATER LAKE	LMB
ULSTER	STURGEON POOL	LMB, SMB, WYE

KEY:

ST	Brook Trout	KOK	Kokanee Salmon
CP	Chain Pickerel	BT	Brown Trout
RT	Rainbow Trout	SMB	Smallmouth Bass
LMB	Largemouth Bass	WYE	Walleye

IMPORTANT:

* PERMIT REQUIRED
ACCESS SITUATIONS VARY WIDELY — INQUIRE AHEAD OF TIME
MANY OF THESE HAVE NOT BEEN SURVEYED RECENTLY;
SPECIES PRESENT COULD BE DIFFERENT

State fishing regulations stand here. The East Sidney Dam Recreation Area, as it's officially called, is open from mid-May to mid-September. You can still fish after this date, but you'd have to find parking outside the facility and walk in. There are separate fees for parking and boating. You can purchase season permits, which at present are $50 per car for parking and $85 per boat. About half of the hundred-odd campsites are seasonals, so if you visit and like the setting, you might want to inquire about this.

Officials here tell me that the primary game fish species is the large-mouth bass. It is quite likely that the severe drawdowns that occur, usually in winter, adversely affect this species, but they say that the fishing is nevertheless quite good. In a DEC survey, smallmouth bass were found to be quite numerous, but that survey was conducted a number of years ago. During full summer pool, the maximum depth of East Sidney is about 50 feet.

There are many special rules in effect, some of them related to fishing. When you check in they will give you sheets enumerating these. You can also call or write to get them in advance.

Don't expect the serene experience you will find on the motorless watershed reservoirs. Still, this could be a good place to bring nonfishing family members, who can swim, waterski, picnic, or explore the landmarks and natural beauty of the northern Catskills.

Other than the watershed reservoirs, East Sidney is the only large stillwater in Delaware County. There are, though, a number of interesting ponds, some of them listed on the chart on page 156.

Ouleout and Charlotte Creeks

These two fairly lengthy streams of the northern Catskills long beckoned to me from several maps I have of the area. Each tracks essentially west into the Susquehanna, and each has a significant branch to the south.

Both streams course through that gorgeous, unspoiled band of Delaware County to the north and west of Route 10 anchored at the ends by Deposit and Stamford. In this magnificent farm country, there isn't a single large town, although there are a number of charming hamlets. The sheer beauty of the area is attraction enough, just so long as you are satisfied on small to medium-sized water.

Ouleout Creek—pronounced o-lee-o—parallels Routes 357, 28, and 14. The cold-water or trout section is that portion above East Sidney Lake, just discussed. Ouleout's main tributary is Treadwell Brook, sometimes called the

There are still many active farms and dairy farms in the northern crescent
of Delaware County. Cows and pastureland provide a soothing backdrop
to a day's fishing in this quiet corner of the world.

Treadwell Branch, or the South Fork of Ouleout Creek. This stream follows
County Route 14.

About 5 miles of Ouleout are stocked, specifically between East Sidney
Reservoir and the junction with the Treadwell Branch. About 2,250 browns
were planted here in a recent season. In addition, several miles of the Treadwell Branch are stocked—900 browns in that same season.

This is not a big river, so the best flows will be encountered below the
meeting of the two branches. This is all private property, and while posting is
not intense, access is tricky. The real problem may not be so much access as
access points. Where a side road heads down to the creek from the main road
there will be a bridge, and from it you can often fish a way upstream or down
(as at the popular Otego Street bridge in Franklin). But there are few such
crosscutting roads, which means a long walk through private property, mostly
farm fields. Out-of-town anglers may not feel comfortable with this situation even if there are no posted signs, but local fishermen tell me that
landowners approached for permission to fish are usually very receptive. If
you travel to fish either Ouleout or Charlotte, plan on at least one day on either stream to orient yourself and find some access, and at least another day
for the actual fishing.

I found some truly exquisite water on the Treadwell Branch, but much posting. Drive east on County Route 14 from the hamlet of Leonta, and look for turns to the left. Follow these down to the stream and see if you can find some unposted water.

Charlotte Creek (see figure 8.1) rises in southwestern Schoharie County, but is located mainly in Delaware County. There is increasing suburban development near the city of Oneonta, though things quiet down east or upstream of Davenport Center. This is another farm stream, but Charlotte doesn't have quite as remote an air as Ouleout, or as intimate a one.

Most of the brown trout stocked here—over 5,000 in a recent season—are planted between Davenport Center and Simpsonville. The same comments made about access to Ouleout Creek would apply here, though unlike on Ouleout, a few state easements do exist. They are not lengthy and are found upstream of Davenport. Corresponding to the situation on Ouleout, the upper waters of Charlotte are quite heavily posted. Brook trout are common in Charlotte Creek and its branches, and are all wild fish. Charlotte's main branch is Kortright Creek, a little smaller than the Treadwell Branch of Ouleout. There is a lot of posting here, though some access may be possible.

Scattered around Delaware County is a whole host of appealing mountain rills, some with engaging names like Handsome Brook, Honest Brook, and Beers Brook. It's probable that wild brook trout and some wild browns exist in all of the dozens of little-fished northern Catskill brooks.

The Small Waters of Schoharie County

Lightly settled Schoharie County is often not included in a discussion of the Catskills, but its southern two-thirds are very mountainous—in fact, more mountainous than that part of Delaware County just discussed. Schoharie's mood and countryside, as well as its geographical postion, clearly ally it to the Catskills, hence its inclusion here.

Fishing opportunities are modest, with no major trout stream and no major public fishing lake except Schoharie Reservoir (see chapter 1). Fishing is largely restricted to small mountain brooks. There are a good many mountains of over 2,500 feet in elevation, and as a result many of those brooks are quite vertical.

There is so much good wild-trout fishing in the Catskills that an angler need not plan an itinerary based on stocking reports. Yet in some ways, state stocking reports do tell a tale. Only one Schoharie stream is stocked with

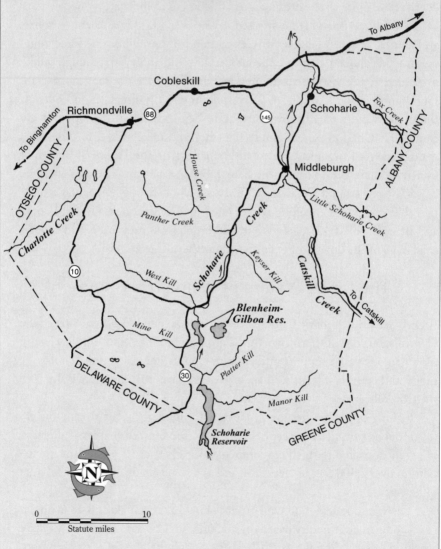

Lower Schoharie County

Figure 8.3

To Albany

To Binghamton

Richmondville

Cobleskill

Schoharie

Fox Creek

ALBANY COUNTY

88

145

OTSEGO COUNTY

House Creek

Middleburgh

Little Schoharie Creek

Charlotte Creek

Panther Creek

Schoharie Creek

Keyser Kill

Catskill Creek

To Catskill

10

West Kill

Blenheim-Gilboa Res.

Mine Kill

DELAWARE COUNTY

30

Platter Kill

Manor Kill

GREENE COUNTY

Schoharie Reservoir

N

0   10
Statute miles

trout. It is the West Kill (not to be confused with Greene County's West Kill), in which were planted 450 brown trout in a recent year. In all the other little brooks of Schoharie County, most or all of the trout taken will be wild fish. Little Schoharie Creek, Panther Creek, Mill Creek, Mine Creek, the Manor Bear Kill—all these and other county streams support wild trout, but they are small brooks, and some will be dry or nearly dry in times of drought.

Schoharie Creek was a large, free-flowing, warm-water river before Schoharie Reservoir came along. As it stands now, there is often little or no spillover from the reservoir so the stream below the dam is in a state of perpetual dry gulch. You have to head fairly far downstream to the point where the tributaries have stitched together a bona fide creek, and here, above and below Middleburgh, it will be almost entirely for warm-water species.

Camping the Catskills

If there's anything better than a Catskill river, it's a Catskill campground where you can wake up to the sound of that river tumbling by. There are dozens of campgrounds in these mountains, many hard to the water's edge but none more than minutes from some type of good fishing.

State campgrounds, all open to the public, are managed by two different agencies. Within the Catskill Park and Adirondack Park boundaries, where all state lands are termed forest preserve, state campgrounds are managed by the New York State Department of Environmental Conservation, whose main address is: DEC, 625 Broadway, Albany, NY 12233. Outside the two forest preserve regions, state campgrounds are managed by the New York State Office of Parks, Recreation and Historic Preservation, Empire State Plaza, Albany, NY 12238. Both offices publish excellent literature, and there is always at least one brochure specifically related to camping reservations. Once you obtain these brochures most of your questions should be answered, but I'll go over a few highlights here.

There are seven state campgrounds within the Catskill Forest Preserve. An eighth, Bear Spring Mountain, is just outside the park boundary and is discussed in this chapter. All are near or on a stream or lake—or both. See the chart on page 162.

Facilities at these state campgrounds vary considerably. Although no forest preserve campgrounds offer water, sewer, or electric hook-ups, all those in the Catskills accommodate RVs and trailers. Trailer length may sometimes be restricted for practical reasons.

Figure 8.4. State campgrounds in the Catskills

NAME OF CAMPGROUND	FACILITIES				WATER WAYS		BOATING			SWIMMING			OTHER		
	TRAILER & TENT SITES	PICNICKING	TRAILER DUMPING STATION	SHOWERS	POND OR LAKE	RIVER OR STREAM	POWER BOATS ALLOWED	ROWBOATS OK – CANOES OK	ROWBOAT OR CANOE RENTAL	SWIMMING	BATH HOUSE	LIFEGUARDS	FISHING	HIKING	HISTORICAL INTEREST
BEAVERKILL, Sullivan County: Off Route 17, 7 miles NW of Livingston Manor. (845) 439-4281	●	●	●	●		●							●	●	●
MONGAUP POND, Sullivan County: Off Route 17, 3 miles N of Debruce. (845) 439-4233	●	●	●	●	●	●		●	●	●	●	●	●	●	
KENNETH L. WILSON, Ulster County: Off Route 28, 4 miles E of Mt. Tremper on Co. Route 40. (845) 679-7020	●	●	●	●	●	●		●	●	●	●	●	●	●	
WOODLAND VALLEY, Ulster County: Off Route 28, 6 miles SW of Phoenicia. (845) 688-7647	●	●	●	●		●							●	●	●
LITTLE POND, Delaware County: Off Route 17, 14 miles NW of Livingston Manor. (607) 439-5480	●	●	●	●	●			●	●	●	●	●	●	●	
DEVIL'S TOMBSTONE, Greene County: Route 214, 4 miles S of Hunter. (518) 688-7160	●	●				●							●	●	●
NORTH/SOUTH LAKE, Greene County: Off Route 23A, 3 miles NE of Haines Falls. (518) 589-5058	●	●	●	●	●			●	●	●	●	●	●	●	●
BEAR SPRING MT. Off Route 206, 5 miles SE of Walton. (607) 865-6989	●	●	●		●	●		●	●	●	●	●	●	●	

AGE REGULATIONS. Camping permits will be issued to anyone 18 years of age or older.

OCCUPANCY. Occupancy is limited to six individuals over the age of twelve years. Site occupancy may be increased by children twelve years of age or under in a party up to the number that the site will accommodate.

Rates at state campgrounds are reasonable, currently $10 to $16 in the forest preserve, with occasional small surcharges for prime waterfront sites. Sites are rented only to people age 18 or older. Many sites and facilities are wheelchair accessible.

Reservations are not required at state campgrounds in the Catskills but are accepted, and are highly recommended on holiday weekends. However, there is a hefty fee—$8.50 at this time—and there are also fees for changing a reservation or for canceling one. My experience has been that these campgrounds are seldom full on weekdays, even in summer, but call the one you're interested in to get a feel for how busy it is. Beginning in 2002, you will be able to reserve individual sites at all the forest preserve campgrounds in the Catskills.

Reservations may be made by mail or phone, but the easiest way is probably via the Internet, at www.ReserveAmerica.com. If you reserve by phone, they will accept Visa or MasterCard.

Private campgrounds abound in the Catskill Mountains. At present, there are about 50 within the core Catskill counties of Delaware, Sullivan, Ulster, and Greene. Some of the more popular ones are on the beautiful Delaware River, where recreational opportunities, including fishing, are the most diverse. Many private "campgrounds" are now little more than trailer parks, and many have no space, or particular affection, for tenters. Many others draw a noisy crowd. Do some homework and know your campground before staying at it.

To locate private campgrounds, first contact the chambers of commerce of the various Catskill counties. They are always churning out nice, information-filled brochures. Another good source is CONY, Campground Owners of New York. This group puts out a lengthy booklet with much information. There are also individual county associations of campground owners. Be sure to keep your eyes peeled for the free, handout brochures that these campground trade associations distribute at tourist gathering points such as supermarkets, sport shops, and historic sites.

Finally, there are a number of national directories of campgrounds found in libraries, in the reference section. A popular one is the Rand McNally guide.

CHAPTER 9

The Delaware— East and West Branches

Much is made about the stages of growth of an angler. First we try to catch as many fish as possible. Then as big a fish as possible. Then as difficult a fish as possible. Then we throw all our fish back. Maybe then we quit fishing altogether and become a Buddhist. It all makes for a fine opening chapter in any one of the endless tumble of literary fly-fishing books written by people who never fished until they were 38.

I've been fishing since I was four, but the East Branch of the Delaware is where I grew up as an angler. Unfortunately, I went right past the Mature Stage to the Dotage Stage, for now I'm most interested in catching . . . edible wild plants! Mayapple in vast groves, wild mint, elberberry, hazelnut—yes, the East Branch is a stream that has it all. This new cause for worry among my family and friends actually has more to do with trout fishing than you might imagine. For one thing, you can still impress people with Latin names (b'jeezus, that's a *Taraxacum officinale,* isn't it?). Not only that, but herbs like wood sorrel and wild leek marry wonderfully with fresh trout. Best of all, if you like to keep a few fish to eat, as I do, you can tell people that you only carry a creel for your forageables. They never guess that under that thick layer of fiddlehead ferns there's a fat Delaware River rainbow.

In this chapter, the East Branch of the Delaware is that section from Pepacton Reservoir down to Hancock (31 miles) and the West Branch of the Delaware is that section from Cannonsville Reservoir down to Hancock (18 miles). I discuss those segments of the Delaware above the reservoirs in other chapters.

East Branch

Before Pepacton Reservoir came along in the 1950s, the East Branch was a large, free-flowing, superlative river, its primary trout water extending down to about Downsville. Almost every year, it would seem, someone would nail a 10-pound-or-better brown. Pepacton wiped out more than 20 miles of the East Branch, but now, with cold-water releases from the reservoir, and through the courtesy of many cold feeder streams, trout habitat extends all the way from the dam at Downsville down to Hancock. There are brown trout both stocked and wild, wild rainbows, and at least a few native brook trout. I know this for a fact, because working above Fish's Eddy one afternoon, I caught all four. I had nailed a few 12- to 14-inch rainbows, and had also caught a few drab, stocked browns along with one gorgeously colored 5-incher that was assuredly a wild fish. Probing the shallow riffle at the head of a large pool, I hooked an 11-inch brook trout. No more than five minutes later I caught a second one, a twin to the first! Quite likely, these brookies were transients from a nearby cold tributary.

A good Catskill fishing story related by Austin Francis centers on a 7-pound brown that Bill Kelly located near the mouth of an East Branch tributary back in the 1950s, before the new road. He tied up an oversized Muddler Minnow and tried for the fish for several days before hooking and ultimately losing it. When he returned the next day, another fisherman was at the spot—hoisting aloft Kelly's fish. The intruder had caught the great brown on a minnow. Francis, in his book *Catskill Rivers,* doesn't specifically state that the tributary was Read Creek, but the whispering is that it was.

There are two quite distinct segments to the East Branch: the upper section from Pepacton down to East Branch village, and the lower section from that point down to Hancock. From here forward, I'll refer to the stream this way. To avoid confusion, when referring to the hamlet of East Branch—as opposed to the river—I'll use the phrase East Branch village.

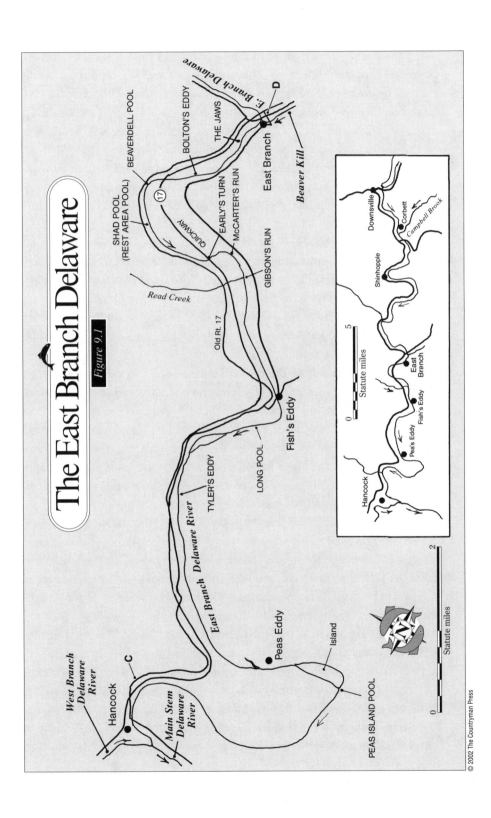

The East Branch Delaware

Figure 9.1

SHAD POOL
(REST AREA POOL)

BEAVERDELL POOL

BOLTON'S EDDY

THE JAWS

E. Branch Delaware

D

East Branch

Beaver Kill

EARLY'S TURN

McCARTER'S RUN

QUICKWAY

17

Read Creek

GIBSON'S RUN

Old Rt. 17

Fish's Eddy

TYLER'S EDDY

LONG POOL

East Branch Delaware River

West Branch Delaware River

Hancock

C

Main Stem Delaware River

Peas Eddy

Island

PEAS ISLAND POOL

Statute miles

0   2

Downsville

Corbett

Campbell Brook

Shinhopple

Statute miles

0   5

East Branch

Fish's Eddy

Pea's Eddy

Hancock

© 2002 The Countryman Press

The upper section is closer to the reservoir and thus runs colder. Browns dominate here, but the extreme upper end, near Downsville, produces an occasional brook trout. The very cold water from under the dam proves accommodating for these brookies, but migration in and out of cold Downs Brook may also have something to do with it. Recently, I've taken wild brookies as far downstream as Shinhopple, and it was already July.

Close friends tell of reliable and heavy Hendrickson hatching on the upper East Branch. You can get the late word on what's hatching at Al's Wild Trout sport shop, located right at the bridge in Shinhopple. He also has nice maps of the East Branch.

Unfortunately, the flow rate at the dam in Downsville is only 95 cubic feet per second (cfs) from June 1 through August 31, 70 cfs in May and September, and just 45 cfs the rest of the year. This means that in a dry year, the water from the dam down to East Branch village is sometimes a little on the thin side, although there are always pools deep enough to shelter trout. With normal rains, this upper section runs at acceptable levels, and is almost always cool enough for trout.

At East Branch village the Beaver Kill enters and, in summer, warms up the East Branch considerably. The bottom end of the Beaver Kill can routinely run in the high 70s, sometimes making it up into the mid-80s for brief periods in the hottest weather. From East Branch village down to Hancock, periodic high water temperatures have a negative impact on the trout fishery. On the other hand, the lower East Branch is a big river, with numerous augmenting tributaries and plenty of deep water at all times in its majestic pools and runs. Yes, it gets a little warm, but the trout seem to ride out the worst days by seeking cold-water refugia in and near the tributaries, by the many cold mountain seeps, and—recent telemetry studies show—by migrating down into the colder West Branch or up into the upper East Branch. When the water level does drop, and assuming the water temperature isn't too high, the worst that usually happens is that some of your favorite riffles become shallow enough to drive you down to the pools.

We East Branch regulars don't want to change a thing. The relatively low water keeps the drift boats somewhat at bay, and the relatively thin density of trout keeps the angling pressure, except at peak times, at a reasonable level.

The biggest East Branch rainbow I've ever caught reinforced two of those key fishing lessons I seem so adept at forgetting.

I was camping at the Red Barn on the main stem around the Fourth of July. It had been extremely hot, but as sometimes happens in these weeks, a rogue cold front blew in and a cold overnight shower and plummeting temperatures chilled local rivers as much as 8 degrees. I had an itch for the East Branch that day, so I drove to a favorite pool and began working a streamer in the fast riffle at the head of a big pool. I had my 19-incher and was back at the campground in time to make breakfast for groggy souls pushing out of their tents.

Lesson one: Go fishing between June and September when a sudden drop in water temperature follows a long hot spell. Lesson two: Big trout that stay hunkered in pools most of the time can be caught with their pants down in the riffle just above the pool.

One expert I spoke with thinks that the rainbow fishery in the East Branch may actually be strengthening, with the fish slightly increasing in size and somewhat increasing in numbers relative to the browns. Is it time to stop stocking brown trout and let this expanding rainbow fishery (remember, they've made it up into the Beaver Kill already) fulfill its apparent destiny? Recent telemetry studies show that there is movement of fish between the branches and between the main stem and the branches. With the main stem and the West Branch both now wild-trout fisheries, couldn't the entire Delaware below the dams be so? There are substantial numbers of wild rainbows in the lower East Branch, some wild brook trout in the upper East Branch, and some wild brown trout down to at least Fish's Eddy. Isn't the river trying to tell us something?

Anglers on some major Catskill rivers are now returning up to 90 percent of the trout they catch, irrespective of the regulations. I think this is another big reason to start swinging management policies further away from stocking and toward wild trout.

The East Branch is never an easy stream. Because so much of the upper-section water is flat and clear, and sometimes a little shallow, the fish are difficult to approach, and long, fine leaders are often necessary. Also, their feeding patterns are unpredictable and the fish just aren't easy to catch. Complicating the problem is the considerable activity in and along the upper East Branch: There are numerous cottages, campgrounds, and clubs, and from them spring forth canoeists and both casual and serious fishermen. There are quieter sections, but you have to hunt them out.

Below East Branch village the fishing is at least as tough, even though there is more forgiving riffle water. First, as I've said, the absolute population of trout in this lower section is just not that great—without doubt, much lower than the now heralded West Branch. Second, the fish seem to be somewhat

A brown just a hair shy of 20 inches, taken in the Delaware River near Hancock.

concentrated in certain sections, although the rainbows definitely skew to the riffles and the browns to the pools. Then there is the two-horned dilemma of fly hatches: They are not especially frequent, yet when a good hatch does materialize, the trout are very selective. I believe the scholarly browns of the Beaver Kill are very selective because of the fishing pressure. On the East Branch, the fish may be selective because the competition from other trout isn't that great. They can take their time in examining an insect, and they may not feel as pressured to feed as would a trout in a more crowded river.

I have fished the lower section of the East Branch many times in every open month, and all of the following hatch information pertains to that lower section.

The best hatches I've seen have been stoneflies (one $2^3/_4$-pound brown I took had 100 nymphs in its stomach), although this is a sporadic hatch sometimes spread out through the whole day; green drakes; sulfurs and other small cream-colored mayflies whose identity I am uncertain of; caddis of several species; and Isonychias. I've never run into a good *Isonychia* hatch here in spring, but I've encountered steady and appealing numbers of one or more species of *Isonychia* in September and on into October. March browns and gray foxes appear in their proper season, but very sporadically by my experience. Right at dark in late June, I've met and fished some wonderfully intense if short-lived hatches of large, light mayflies—probably either *Stenonema* or *Potamanthus*. This action likely continues into July.

There are often heavy grannom caddis hatches *(Brachycentrus numerosus)* in spring. Near Fish's Eddy, one angling buddy experienced not only a thick grannom hatch but a good rise of trout to it as well. This is seldom the case with this superabundant early-season Catskill hatch. As on other nearby rivers, that dark, early-June caddis can make a fantastic showing here. Sometimes there are two dark caddis on the water together—one about size 12 to 14, and the other about size 16. Once at McCarter's it took me all evening to unravel this common complex hatch, but the reward was an 18-inch brown just before dark.

One time while walking downstream I noticed a kind of dust on the banks and at the edge of the river. Closer inspection revealed that it was not dust at all but green drake nymph shucks. Millions of them! To hit this hatch, try the last four days of May and the first six of June. The "coffin fly" spinners come down a few days later, but often in faster water. Sometimes the trout come up to these big, tempting imagoes and sometimes they don't. When they do, it will be the best dry-fly action you'll ever see on the lower

East Branch. As for that dust, be on the watch for it, because top-flight green drake hatching may be occurring just upstream of where you find it.

When the shad run is a good one in the main Delaware, these anadromous gamesters may also be plentiful in the East Branch. Anglers see them all the way up to the dam at Downsville, but almost all the effort for shad takes place below East Branch village. While shad are schooling fish, they disperse very well, and you can catch them in both the riffles and the pools. On the lower East Branch there is one very well-known pool that is in fact called the Shad Pool. Also a good place to encounter green drakes, it's a long, silt-bottomed run located behind the rest area (and is therefore also called the Rest Area Pool); it's accessible from the westbound lanes of the Quickway. You can park at the rest area and walk down to the stream. I have also caught shad in the big pool below McCarter's Run and in Fish's Eddy both at the bridge and in the large pool just below the bridge. Although it may not seem too scientific, many shad lovers simply look off a Delaware River bridge to see if any shad are visible. Then they decide whether it's trout or shad that day. Below Fish's Eddy there are a number of long pools or eddies where this silvery, hard-fighting, porpoising herring may be tangled with. As far as technique goes, that is discussed in chapter 10. The East Branch is not nearly as popular for shad as is the main stem.

Smallmouth bass are very much present in the East Branch, though I've seldom gotten one worth catching, let alone taking home. Once I caught a 12-incher at The Jaws, and it honestly looked twice as big as any other smallmouth I'd taken in the East Branch.

Walleyes are present in the entire lower East Branch below East Branch village. I've never gotten one—not that I've really tried for them here—but if I were to target this species, I would look for them on the bottom in the deeper, slower pools, as discussed more fully in the next chapter. Although I am not here drawing any conclusions from it, in one DEC July survey on the lower East Branch, they actually saw more walleyes than trout.

Access to the East Branch of the Delaware is still quite good. There is admittedly much human activity and some posting on the upper section. You can take advantage of some of this by staying at the campgrounds found here, and even renting their canoes to fish the water. When you stay at such a river's-edge campground, you—along with the other guests—almost always get a private beat of water to fish. There are also several miles worth of easements, including a fairly new one below the bridge at Shinhopple. The Wild Trout sport shop, mentioned above, has a small parking lot for sports who want to give this stretch a whirl. As far as the lower East Branch goes, a good portion of this 13-mile stretch is open to the public due to state easements. East Branch easements can be found on a map titled "Fishing Delaware County," available at http://www.delawarecounty.org.

West Branch

Now I know why God created the West Branch of the Delaware: to keep people away from the places that I like to fish by myself. The Mongaup River, the Little Beaver Kill, Oquaga Creek, a couple of hundred brook trout streams—they're all empty now, and God bless the West Branch! Small trout just don't sate the modern angler.

But almost everyone is more sociable than I am, so if you want to catch some really nice trout and don't mind the crowds, this is the stream for you. In fact, no less than the Caucci-Nastasi fishing team made this statement in a magazine article: "The upper Delaware River System is one of the best wild trout fisheries in the country, and its West Branch is the crown jewel of that system." One state biologist agreed with my contention that this may be the best trout stream in New York State.

Before Cannonsville Dam was completed in 1963, West Branch trout ran down only about as far as Deposit. Thus, the section we're discussing here was once primarily a warm-water fishery, noted for its smallmouth bass and walleye fishing. Cold water released from the bottom of Cannonsville now makes the West Branch suitable for trout for its entire length.

From Cannonsville Dam downstream about 1.5 miles to the low Stilesville Dam, New York City has enacted a no-fishing, no-entrance policy, so the West Branch for anglers runs about 16 miles from the Stilesville Dam down to Hancock.

The extensive DEC-secured easements that exist on much of the lower Beaver Kill and on some of the East Branch are not found here. There are only a few short ones. But while the banks on both sides are primarily in private hands, and posting is fairly heavy, I'd still call access good overall. The water right around Deposit, good water (yes, I do fish this stream sometimes), is mostly unposted and provides fine opportunity. There is free water, too, at the Stilesville dam, where some very large trout are taken. In fact, if you were after a wall-hanger, this is one of the first places (considering only rivers) that I would send you to in the Catskills. A fine place to fish is just below the Quickway bridge at Deposit, where you'll find a long, productive

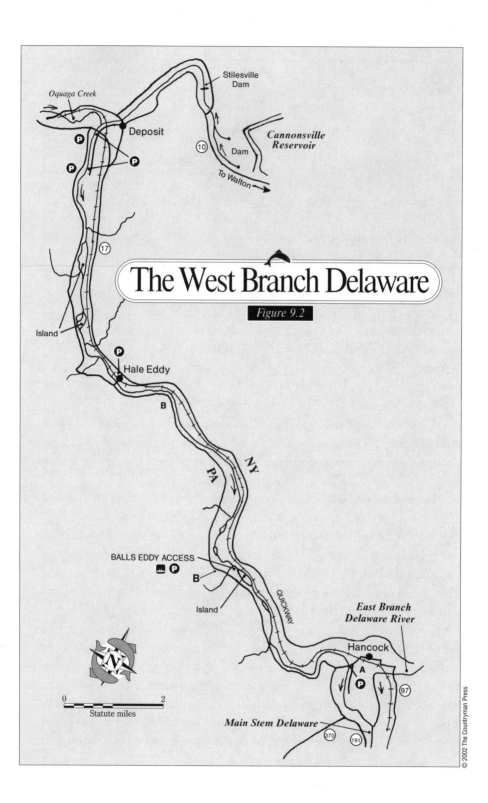

The West Branch Delaware

Figure 9.2

Oquaga Creek

Stilesville
Dam

Deposit

Cannonsville
Reservoir

10

Dam

To Walton

17

Island

Hale Eddy

B

NY

PA

BALLS EDDY ACCESS

B

Island

QUICKWAY

East Branch
Delaware River

Hancock

A

P

97

N

0   2

Statute miles

Main Stem Delaware

370   191

The low Stilesville Dam a mile or two below the main Cannonsville Dam.
While the entire West Branch is highly productive, and many of its pools
harbor big trout, this is one of the best places to try for a fish of over 20 inches.

pool and some minipools and runs created by a small island there. One year I
fished to an unbelievable Hendrickson hatch at this pool. The April 27 hatch
started in early afternoon and seemed to go on forever, with heavy hatching
continuing well into the evening. It is no-kill from the big Route 17 bridge
downstream 2 miles. This is the place to bring your client.

From Deposit downstream to a point about 1 mile below Hale Eddy, it's
still New York State property on both sides of the river. On the west side,
there is a local road called River Road, and on it, as shown on the map, there
are two angler's parking lots just a short way below Deposit. These give you
access to some highly productive water. The rest of the west bank down to
Hale Eddy is mostly posted. Be sure to ask permission before crossing private lands, here and elsewhere.

On the east side of this upper part of the West Branch, the Quickway
borders the river, with wide farm fields often separating the two. Along the
no-kill reach just below Deposit, there are two angler's parking areas. Below
this, the river is sometimes close to the Quickway and in view, and sometimes just out of sight. Some anglers do park along the Quickway, but with
Route 17 soon to become Interstate 86, it's unclear whether or not this is still
going to work. For the time being, try to use the established pull-offs where

your car will be well out of the traffic lane. Reports are that anglers have been ticketed in the past for parking along the Quickway. Alas, most of the east bank from Deposit down to Hale Eddy is private, although some ambitious anglers do find legitimate access points and then use the train tracks to walk up- or downstream.

One bona fide access point is right at the Hale Eddy bridge, which can be reached from the eastbound lane and—for the time being—also from the westbound lane of the Quickway. There is enough parking for a number of cars in a small lot just east of the bridge by the still-active railroad tracks. There is excellent water right at the bridge and for a good way upstream, where a cold tributary comes on board. If you like quiet, challenging water for dry-fly fishing, you'll like the pool that starts at the bridge and extends several hundred yards downstream. As this pool tails out, it becomes ever more still, but it maintains depth, and looking downstream off the bridge rising trout are sometimes visible for as far as the eye can see. There is also some beautiful water just about a mile upstream of Hale Eddy.

Not far below Hale Eddy on the west side is the West Branch Angler, a full-service fly-fishing resort that offers not only a private beat of water for guests, but also lodging, meals, a well-stocked tackle shop, and guide service. Just a bit farther downstream the Pennsylvania border first touches the river, and it is Pennsylvania turf on the west bank from here down to Hancock. Luckily, along this stretch the commonwealth of Pennsylvania owns a number of miles of riverbank. Hunting with a Pennsylvania license is allowed on the land (State Game Land 299) along this stretch of river, and fishing in the river with either a New York or Pennsylvania fishing license is also allowed. Signs clearly define the extent of this public water, but you must park in established lots. The walk down to the river through hickory groves and sunny meadows is reward in itself, and the length of the walk tends to reduce the number of anglers.

In addition, Pennsylvania has a nice access point at Balls Eddy, shown on figure 9.2. There is a very good launch ramp for canoes or drift boats here, along with some very nice water upstream, downstream, and right at this ramp, although the many weekend warriors who casually give this beat a whirl must have the trout pretty jaded by now. There is plenty of parking, although overnight parking is forbidden, and once again either a Pennsylvania or a New York fishing license is acceptable. A wonderful float trip would be from the Ball's Eddy access down to the Buckingham access on the Delaware's main stem. This would allow you to fish some fine water on the

An excellent, well maintained access site on the West Branch is the one at Ball's Eddy, on the Pennsylvania side. There is a good boat launch and plenty of parking. Many guides running drift boats will start here and take their sports down through part of the upper main stem.

West Branch and the best trout section on the main stem. It is, in fact, the float that many guides prefer. See the essay near the end of chapter 10.

A week before this was written, biologists did some sampling at Ball's Eddy and caught six striped bass up to 28 inches in length (no bluefish). Over on the East Branch, striped bass have now been seen at least as far upriver as the rest area on Route 17, which is just about a mile from the Beaver Kill. This recent phenomenon of stripers in the upper Delaware, which one expert considers a potential threat to the trout, is discussed a little further in chapter 10.

Al Caucci's Delaware River Club is on the Pennsylvania side a short way upstream from Hancock. One of the most spectacular pools on the river falls within its holdings, and this pool is in fact used for the fly-fishing instruction that the club offers. It also offers campsites, lodging, meals, guide service, drift-boat trips, and a small tackle shop.

Because of the way water is released from the reservoir, conditions on the West Branch are somewhat strange. There isn't nearly enough space here to go into a full discussion of water-release policies from the Catskill reservoirs, let alone even a brief history of those policies. I'll try to just cover a few of the highlights as they relate to fishermen.

Since summer is when cold water is most important for protecting the trout in the West Branch and the main stem below it, the heaviest regular releases—160 cubic feet per second (cfs)—are made between June 1 and September 15. What's called a "thermal stress bank" is held in reserve in Cannonsville Reservoir so that releases even greater than 160 cfs can be made on very hot days when water temperatures reach a level damaging to trout. Thus, if you come here between June 1 and September 15 you will usually find water levels acceptable, even a little high. But don't try to figure out in advance what the water level is going to be. Several other factors can affect that, including heavy rains that swell the river naturally, spillover from Cannonsville when the reservoir is full, or requests for water from the Delaware "River Master" who, via a 1954 Supreme Court decree, is empowered to demand water from various reservoirs on the watershed to maintain a flow of 1,750 cfs at Montague, New Jersey (widely known as the Montague Formula).

Because of all these variables, you can often come here and find a flow of 300 to 600 cfs, the top figure being about the biggest that the wade fisherman can negotiate. Bigger "bubbles" of up to and over 1,000 cfs occur. The drift-boat operators will usually sail with a release of 400 but are not put off by the bigger releases. The guides really don't want to spend a lot of time dragging the boat. The main stem is of course bigger water, and floatable a much higher percentage of the time than is the West Branch.

On the other hand, drought conditions can allow New York City to legally tighten up on releases (the River Master cannot be overruled), which means that you can come to the West Branch at almost any time and find low water.

From April 1 through May 31—opening day on the West Branch varies by section—the release is only 45 cfs. This is not necessarily a big negative. In fact, it's sometimes nice to see a Catskill river low and clear at a time when high, roily water is more the rule. But this is not something to depend on either. On April 1 the dam is usually spilling, and heavy rains can quickly bring the West Branch up in these normally wet spring months. Nonetheless, right from the gun in April, both fly- and spin-anglers do well on browns that run up to 20 inches and better. In fact, one April 20 I fished the West Branch when the thermometer had hit an amazing 90 degrees. With the low water and intense heat, it felt like midsummer, but 20 or so chunky browns came to net on that sweltering day. I was never uncomfortable in my waders, because of the extremely cold water.

While you can never exactly predict West Branch or main-stem water levels, you can find out exactly how high the water is at any given moment: Just go to the U.S. Geological Survey web site listed on page 211.

From September 16 to the close of the regular season on September 30—the part of the West Branch bordering Pennsylvania is open year-round on a no-kill basis—the West Branch is again subjected to that low cfs figure. Yet I've found the last two weeks of September to be one of the best times to fish here. The autumn rains normally come by mid-September, and this can perk up the river and make it very appealing at this time. Hatches can be surprisingly strong and varied in these beautiful late-summer and early-autumn weeks.

Finally, understand that the river is about 18 miles long. The closer to the dam you are at any given time, the lower the water and, usually, the colder the water. The closer you get to Hancock, the greater the height of the river due to the contributions of several tributaries and, usually, the warmer the water, although it seldom goes above 65 degrees Fahrenheit.

Now that you're informed about West Branch realities, you can start to plot a few strategies.

One Fourth of July weekend some friends and I got to Deposit and found the water at 46 degrees—typical, during releases, for the upper fourth of the river. After two hours of futile casting, I decided to head downstream to look for some warmer water and, hopefully, more active trout. My friends stuck it out near Deposit. My hunch paid off, for while my pals did very little upstream, I took five fish, including one rainbow of about 17 inches. I was fishing just above Hancock, where the water was 60 degrees right on the button.

It's been my experience that good fly hatches start a little earlier here in spring than on other Catskill rivers. Not only that, but good rises of trout also seem to start earlier, and I can only theorize why this is so. It could be that there are just so many trout that competition requires the fish to take advantage of nearly every surface event. Then, too, it might be because the West Branch fish are conditioned by the cold releases so that they are unusually active during the cold temperatures of early spring. Whatever the reason, this is the first Catskill river I would head to in April if I wanted to jump the gun on the dry-fly season. It can also be a good summertime stream for the trout fisherman, with excellent hatches occurring intermittently throughout the summer. Overall, though, May and September may be the top months for dry-fly fishermen.

As I mentioned earlier, I have timed some truly fine Hendrickson

Because of the very cold water, a mist often hangs over the West Branch during the warmer months. Farm fields stretch back to the enchanting hills and valleys of the Catskills.

hatches here over the years. The *Ephemerella subvaria* duns ordinarily promote excellent surface activity, but the bigger fish are seldom easy. Realistic patterns are often necessary, although there have been many times when a size 14 Adams has bailed me out during this and other Delaware River hatches. Also in fairly early spring, there will be some caddis and some stoneflies buzzing about, and you may even see some of the classic quill Gordons *(Epeorus pleuralis)* that seem to have regrettably dwindled on many other Catskill rivers. Then, after the early-season flies, the gap is often filled by other *Ephemerella* mayflies, and by the little blue-winged olives (sizes 18 through 24) that are so pervasive and so important on numerous Catskill rivers. From early June into early July, two species of "drakes" may appear. These are the green *(Ephemera guttulata)* and the brown *(E. simulans)*. Then, too, from mid-June through early July the sulfur hatch can provide superb late-day, evening, and sometimes even afternoon fishing. According to Al Caucci and Bob Nastasi, two lesser-touted mayflies, *Ephemerella deficiens* and *Heptagenia hebe,* may be seen on the West Branch anytime from mid-July through October.

From the Stilesville dam down to below Deposit, firm-flanked browns inured to the cold water hold sway. These once-caught, twice-shy selective trout average a healthy 11 to 13 inches, and many 14- to 18-inch fish enliven the day for the skillful. Ten years ago I never saw a rainbow in this upper end, but I have taken a few in recent seasons, including one of 16 inches near Oquaga Creek. Paralleling the situation below the Neversink and Pepacton dams, there are a few smartly-colored brookies in the upper West Branch—perhaps even the length of the river. Somewhere below Hale Eddy, rainbows become a bit more numerous, and are an important part of the mix at Hancock, although even here browns are considerably more numerous. While browns of 10 pounds and better probably exist in the West Branch, it's almost certain that fish over 6 pounds are caught every year.

Some Flowery Predictions

You need not turn to a textbook to know when this or that hatch is about to take place. The clues are everywhere—in the trees and shrubs, in the movements of the animals, and, most of all, in the appearance of the Catskill wildflowers.

The lovely spring beauty appears just in time to see the first stirrings of insect life along the banks of the Beaver Kill–Delaware River system. A few stoneflies here, a few caddis there, a lucky encounter with a blue-winged olive on another pool—this is early spring in the mountains.

The spring beauty is a delicate, subtle flower, white petaled with rich, pink veins. Sometimes called fairy spuds, it has an edible tuber that's like a potato but much smaller—only about the size of a nickel. In the stony Catskill soil, it's often difficult to extract, but anyway, who would have the heart to excavate such a pretty little flower?

The coltsfoot, like some other early flowers, comes into full bloom before the greenery of the plant has developed. With no leaves to obscure the blossoms, the effect can be stunning, especially since coltsfoot often grows in thick clumps. Now is the time when quill Gordons will emerge in those colder, purer streams that are still capable of nurturing this delicate mayfly.

This year I saw my first little blue quill on the same day that I spotted my first trout lily. Sometimes called dogtooth violet, this yellow flower is very inconspicuous, and it is easy to look right past. On this same day I noticed a strange plant growing in thin stalks, each stalk possessing two slight, bulbous protrusions. I later discovered that it was horsetail—which, when fully grown, was used by pioneers to clean pots. It turns out that the thin leaves of this plant are embedded with silica! There were catkins on the poplars this day, and pine siskins at Murray's bird feeders.

There is a very light-colored, large caddis (size 12) that I've been observing on the Beaver Kill in recent seasons. This year its appearance coincided with my first stumble upon foamflower. Sometimes called false miterwort, it has a leaf somewhat like a flowering red raspberry (though much smaller), and the tightly grouped white flowers have very long stamens. If you squint, you can imagine foam rather than individual little flowers, though I can't say if that explains the common name.

Often the first gaudy showing of dame's rocket will coincide with the very first green drakes on the Delaware. Almost everybody calls this tall, showy flower phlox, but it's actually in the mustard family, and has only four petals instead of five like phlox. There are stalks with pink flowers and stalks with white flowers, and often, groupings of each will be growing together. This season, for the first time, I saw a stalk that had flowers made up of both deep pink and white petals. This created a striking effect.

Just as the green drakes are passing and the bright-bodied Ephemerella cornutas are making an appearance, the developing fernlike foliage of yarrow will be observed. Pinch a piece and place it next to your nose. It's highly scented. The off-white to slightly purplish flower head will bloom in another week and a half. Like coltsfoot, this is a medicinal herb of ancient application.

You may see the first sulfurs on the West Branch just when the yellow goatsbeard opens its striking yellow flower head. This flower has long, grasslike leaves, and the juice of the stem is milky. It's a morning person, its flowers closing up shop by midday, long before those pretty pale evening duns start to rise deliberately over the quieter runs. Closely related to salsify, it has a tuber that's edible at certain times.

About this time, too, the evidence of spittlebugs will reach its peak. The nymph of this insect, which is also called a froghopper, surrounds itself with a foamy mass, for reasons that have not yet been revealed to me. Mugwort is one common alien plant that the spittlebug seems to favor.

Many fly-fishers miss some excellent early-morning hatching. It doesn't just occur in late season. If the weather's been hot, morning hatches can even occur in midseason. When you notice that the purplish red Juneberries (the fruit of the shadbush) are fully ripe, you may see small, size 16 blue-winged olives on the river. They appear about 8 or 9 o'clock. This year, after the hatch had waned, I stopped and gathered a pint of the berries and later composed a batch of sourdough Juneberry muffins.

In just a few days, you will see musk mallow—its notched leaves are un-mistakable—as well as butter-and-eggs, common mullein, and the very first scanty and scattered blooms of the spotted touch-me-not. Now you should look for some sporadic daytime hatches of stoneflies, and for some interesting evening hatches that may include *Ephemerella dorothea* or *Isonychia* spinners, two different dark gray caddisflies, and perhaps other flies as well.

About the time the textbooks say the mayfly hatches are largely over, I look for a surprising but as-yet-unidentified size 14 blue-winged olive on the East Branch of the Delaware. My clues as to its arrival? The striking red bee balm will now be in full bloom, and the exquisitely colored Canada lilies will be hiding among the husky boneset and tall river grass just where the river-bank meets the wide floodplain. Now is when the wild raspberries will be growing in surfeit in any sunny spot along the river. The best of the hatches have come and gone, and high summer is upon the Catskills.

CHAPTER 10

The Delaware River

When the East and West Branches meet at Hancock, one of America's great rivers is born. But here on the Delaware proper, an angler used to 30-foot-wide streams can easily feel overwhelmed. There are pools—"eddies" in the Delaware vernacular—that can stretch to a thousand yards. There are places where the river itself is hundreds of yards wide. There are also steep embankments where one has to gingerly clamber down over rocks that are foot-loose and reported to harbor timber rattlesnakes. The main stem of the Delaware is not for everyone.

Despite these obstacles, though, and despite occasionally lethal water temperatures and a growing armada of watercraft of all types, there are trout here, trout that average an honest 15 to 16 inches.

A long time ago the Delaware held natural populations of shad in-season, along with eel and some panfish. I did not consult historical records to see if there might also have been early runs of migratory striped bass, or even other species. Both smallmouth bass and rainbow trout were apparently introduced in the late 1800s. The rainbows were reportedly implanted to several feeders of the Delaware, among them Callicoon Creek. The 'bows thrived in these New York and Pennsylvania streams for 80-odd years, though all the while most of the main river remained too warm for them. Those initial plantings provided the seed stock for today's Delaware rainbow fishery.

Right now the upper main Delaware would still be a warm-water river

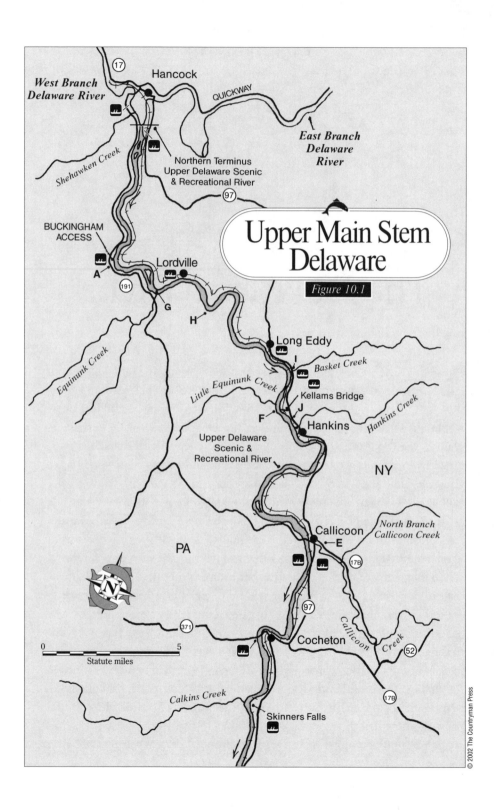

© 2002 The Countryman Press

were it not for the cold releases from the city reservoirs. It was Pepacton releases that first made possible a trout zone in the main Delaware. At that time, in the late 1950s and early to mid-1960s, these cold releases allowed trout to live at least as far down as Long Eddy. But then the bulk of the releases started coming from Cannonsville, which is closer, and the trout zone was extended down to about Callicoon. From that point downstream, it is principally a warm-water fishery, with shad the primary target followed by smallmouth bass and walleyes. Still, even downstream of Callicoon trout are caught, especially in spring near the mouths of the colder streams. A reliable acquaintance of mine specifically fishes for and catches large browns in the lower main stem, well below Callicoon, and he takes them even in summer. He likes to fish at night with flashy spoons.

Despite these stray, downstream salmonids, there are quite clearly two sections to the main stem from the fisherman's point of view. I'll talk first about the primary trout water, that zone from Hancock down to approximately Callicoon.

There is one very happy coincidence on the main Delaware: The best canoe water is below Callicoon. This lessens river traffic in the trout zone. Of course canoeists can and do float from Hancock down, and even in the East and West Branches. But below-average rainfall can make this upstream mileage really bony, and beyond that, downriver sections offer more rapids to add spice to the game. In the terrible drought summer of 1985, the Delaware was so low that canoe traffic came to a grinding halt above Callicoon. Trout fishermen had the river to themselves, though some also had the trauma of seeing thermal fish kills here and in the West Branch. This event helped to spur activism for the more favorable release patterns that exist today.

Even when the water is up, weekdays aren't bad at all with canoe traffic. Before June 15, it's very light on the upper part of the main stem, even on weekends. Between then and Labor Day, there still is little traffic on weekdays, though weekends can be busy. Canoe traffic is extremely heavy on the Fourth of July weekend, and also Memorial Day weekend.

Anglers must now also share the river with—themselves. There are now about 55 to 60 licensed river guides, about double the number of five years ago. Most run fishing trips with drift boats in the trout zone, but some drift below Callicoon. Many anglers are also bringing their own drift boats, not to mention canoes. Then there is that relatively new phenomenon, the belly boat, an individual flotation device. These are used primarily on the upper main stem and also a bit on the West Branch. No, solitude is no longer the

A familiar scenario on the main stem: The river is up and wading is next to impossible. Angler Tony Apollonio reaches out with his punchy 7-weight outfit. Good casting skills will serve you well on the Big D.

reason for visiting the main stem of the Delaware, where I could once fish a certain riffle near my campsite and not see anyone for hours at a stretch.

Overall in the main stem, rainbows seem to outnumber browns by a substantial margin. At Hancock, and for a few miles downstream, browns may be about as numerous as rainbows. But below Lordville, my own experience is that rainbows are as much as eight times as plentiful as browns. Unfortunately, I could find no scientific substantiation of this. One expert thinks that the browns may be more difficult to catch—because they're warier in general and also because they relate more heavily to the pools—and therefore may be somewhat more numerous than personal experience would tend to indicate.

Most of the main-stem trout are wild. There is no stocking. Still, a significant number of hatchery browns probably drift or migrate down from the East Branch or from other tributaries that are stocked. Doubtless, a few wanderlust brookies from any of a score of cold mountain rills appear from time to time in the main stem. I have never caught any, though. Despite all the spirited stories about 5- and 6-pound rainbows, there is strong evidence that 22 inches is about the biggest they typically get to be here; this may be a genetic limitation. One biologist netted a fish that just made that length, and it was thin and deteriorating.

Hatches on the main stem can be very strong, but seem to be more diverse and impressive between Hancock and Lordville than below Lordville. Complex hatches, with more than one insect on the water, are very common.

As on the East Branch, there is an excellent population of big stoneflies in the main stem. Best hatching time is May to mid-July, but the nymphs are in the river and no doubt taken by trout most of the year. Nymph fishing is never easy on this big water, but if nymphing is something you've cultivated, bring along some stonefly imitations. There are also plenty of caddis. In fact, caddis stick larvae and stonefly nymphs are what you seem to find most of under and around Delaware River rocks. A wet fly that can take trout, walleyes, and bass is a Woolly Bugger in sizes 6 to 10. This fly is highly touted by some Delaware River guides.

While you may encounter caddis in a variety of sizes and shades, mayflies are also very important. As on the Beaver Kill, there can be some pulse-raising early-season activity with Hendricksons and little blue quills, which frequently are on the water together. There is no way to know exactly when this activity will commence, but I'd say the peak period would be between about April 25 and May 7, depending on weather conditions. Main-stem trout are very selective, and that goes for the Hendrickson hatch. In the quieter runs, realistic patterns are essential. Be sure to have emerger patterns and floating nymphs, too. In a pinch, a dry fly can be clipped back to create the impression of an emerging mayfly. One year my friend Tony gave me a trailing-shuck Hendrickson dry and within 10 minutes I hooked a big rainbow with it.

The lull following the early-season activity can be profound, and its duration is exaggerated when the weather is warm and the Hendricksons come and go on the early side. Caddisflies and small blue-winged olives may appear almost anytime, but in those middle weeks of May you can, in some years, visit this river days on end without seeing more than a couple of rising fish. What to do? The best approach is to float the river: If fish aren't rising on one pool, they may be on the next. Of course, drifting with a guide is not inexpensive, so wading anglers outnumber those in boats by a wide margin.

On the Beaver Kill and many other nontailwaters you can almost always drum up some fish by blind fishing a dry fly between mid-May and mid-June, when the water temperature is about perfect for trout. But blind casting drys on the Big D is another matter altogether. The devout nymph fisherman will ply his craft during these quiet weeks but, as for me, I'd rather see some fish rising on this tough river. That's when I sometimes become a "road hunter," driving from access point to access point hoping to find risers. River guides also don't like to have their guests expend a lot of time fishing blind. They would rather move on down to find risers, although every guide will have pet spots where nonrising fish can often be drummed up. Good guides also have lots of hunches—cast where they tell you to.

As May wears on and the productive midseason period approaches, the chance of encountering a good hatch increases. Daytime activity is possible, and the chance for an evening rise gets better and better as June 1 nears.

One evening while readying myself for some anticipated coffin fly excitement, I was standing on a high bank overlooking the river when an extraordinary number of March brown *(Stenonema vicarium)* spinners began to buzz around me. I've never seen many of the duns of this species on the Big D, but that spinner flight in late May sure put me on the lookout for them.

The March brown's sister fly—the gray fox *(S. fuscum)*—has also been reported in good numbers on the main stem, but I've not personally encountered any great numbers of this pretty mayfly.

As evening activity intensifies toward late May and into early June, you start to become aware that there is also a lot of small stuff on this river—midges, microcaddis, and tiny blue-winged olive mayflies.

And there is big stuff, too. The green drake hatch can be impressive on the main stem, but I've found that it's the green drake spinner—not the dun—that makes for the best fishing. Green drake hatch dates can never be predicted with certainty, but I look for them anytime from May 25 to about June 10.

If the spring weather is more or less normal, with average rainfall and temperatures, I'll expect to find some evening activity here during the first 10 days of June. But if the weather is particularly hot and dry, the "midseason" hatches seem to come early, and June can take on a dead, summerlike quality.

No fly-fishing season in the Catskills is exactly like any other season. With the main stem, more than with any other river I know, you have to put in your time to hit those periods when it all comes together. As I've said, by floating the river you swing the odds in your favor. It also helps to fish on cloudy days, which almost always produce better hatching and better fishing, especially in summer.

The most prolonged hatch I've seen here is a blue-winged olive of about

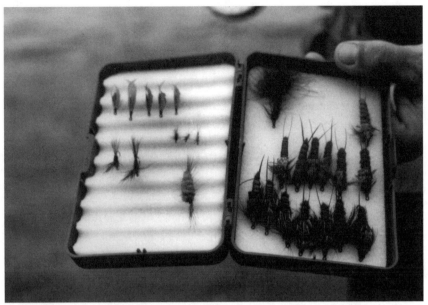

Big stonefly patterns are in the vests of all serious main stem fly fishermen.
It's often the first thing turned to when no hatches are to be seen.

a size 18 or 20. It seems to hatch all day, and I have seen it often in June and July. In truth, I don't know what exact species this is. Most likely, there are several different blue-winged olive species present during this time frame, and on some days I have seen two or three different sizes of blue-wings on the water at the same time. Stream studies done by biologists with Penn State University do show the presence of great numbers of *Baetis* nymphs here.

As far as bait-fishing goes, a skilled bait-angler will always take fish, anywhere. But the extreme rockiness of the Delaware makes bottom fishing with bait difficult. Nonetheless, this didn't seem to stop two anglers I ran into.

The first one was walking up from a riffle where I planned to fly-cast the last hour before darkness. He had been fishing worms downstream through an especially rocky string of riffles, and had taken five rainbows averaging 14 inches.

"How do you hack all those rocks?" I asked him.

"You just have to like tying," he grinned. "The people at the local tackle shop love me!"

That same week I was tubing down near Hankins when I passed a man with an extremely short spinning rod in his hand. The rod was bent over double.

"What's that on there?" I yelled to him.

"Big trout," he said, not seeming to be overly excited.

"Whatcha hook him on?" I followed, as I started to float beyond comfortable ear range.

"Stonefly nymph," he said, just as the rod went straight and the fish got off.

When I got down to my campsite I got out of my tube and walked upstream, curious about this man fishing a fly with a spinning rod.

"No," he told me. "I'm using live nymphs. I dig them up in the rocks."

"What have you caught so far this weekend?" I pressed him.

"A 14-incher and a 17-incher."

Shortly after that, I found out that it is illegal to take nymphs (and other aquatic insects) from trout streams in New York. But fear not: The man apparently had an epiphany, because I met him a few years later and now he fishes only with flies. His favorite pattern? Stonefly nymphs!

Still on the subject of bait, some local pros are fond of fishing live shiners for both trout and walleyes. A boat or canoe helps enormously here, since you can drift through the deeper pools and pretty well avoid the snags that you inevitably would encounter if shore fishing.

You can be mesmerized—and you should be—by the fecund beauty of the floodplain of the Delaware, where the chance to observe deer, turkeys, wood ducks, beavers, snakes, turtles, wildflowers, and myriad other things is ever present. But when you step down to the water's edge, the hard cold truth is that the deck will be stacked against you. The big Delaware offers a Ph.D. in trout fishing, but it's a long, hard program. If you go with a guide, you will be benefiting from his hundreds of days on the river, not to mention the many miles you will cover in the course of the day. Fishing on your own, especially without a boat, will prove a major challenge. Knowing and meeting the better hatches is, of course, profitable. But knowing how to approach this large river is of more primary importance. So let's talk about Main-Stem Strategy 101.

Often you'll get here and find no fish working, or only a few. Think of it as par for the course. For one thing, the absolute population of trout in the river (except near Hancock) is just not that great. But look hard. There may be a few hungry fish coming up that you didn't notice right away. Don't start making mental comparisons to other smaller rivers where, during a good hatch, rising trout are visible up and down the stream. Be satisfied with just a few risers, and then go after them.

It's often said that, during the green drake hatch, you should pick out just one good fish and make that fish your evening's work. I'd say that should be your approach on the main stem all the time. Don't thrash about wildly. Carefully approach the river, carefully wade, carefully observe what's on the water, and then carefully choose a fish. Most often, it will be a fish over 14 inches—and it will be both easily put down and often quite selective.

Cast a lot less on the main stem, and be more thoughtful about it. This is not the West Branch, or the Willowemoc. Expect the trout to reject your offering. Then think about what you can do to make that not happen just a few times in four hours of fishing.

You have to assess the activity. If there are only one or two risers, go right to one of them. One-rise wonders are painfully common here. Not only that, but they seem to move around more than feeding trout on other, smaller rivers.

One June during the "black lady" hatch, my name for a very common dark caddis, I worked over what I came to call a "wolf pack" of large rainbows all rising together in a small section of water near shore. This type of activity is seldom written about, but experts tell me it isn't especially uncommon. Clearly, these bruisers were taking the floating caddis, and they were moving upriver as they fed, staying very close to shore. I must have followed them nearly 100 yards upstream, and it was almost dark before one of them finally took my Henryville Special. The fish raced for the middle of the river and soon had all the fly line in the air. Now the backing raced out and all I could do was hold on to the rod. I'm usually very careful about knots but apparently not this time, since the backing came off the reel arbor. Somehow, the bitter end of the backing caught on the tip-top of the rod and I quickly grabbed it. I started playing the fish with just the line, but in only a few seconds the fly popped out of the trout's mouth. When I come to the main stem now, I make sure that my reel has at least 150 yards of backing.

If the hatch is strong—and it almost always takes a strong one to bring up fish in numbers—then you can be a little more patient. When I'm blessed with the rare serendipity of six or eight or more fish feeding in sight of me, I like to hold back until one of them gets into what Caucci and Nastasi call "a greedy feeding rhythm." When I feel a particular fish is "ready," then and only then will I cast to it. On this river, especially, I put much weight on that first cast. Still, it has to be the right pattern and the right presentation.

A 3-foot seine is survival gear on the main stem. Carry it down from the car, all the time. Anyone can spot those gaudy duns or restless sedges, but it's what you can't see on the Big D that can hurt you. Especially study the seine

Foot access to the East and West Branches is relatively good, but that's not true on the trout section of the main stem. A canoe helped us to get at that nice but relatively inaccessible stretch between Hancock and Long Eddy.

for small emergers, drowned duns or caddis, very small flies, and other morsels that the trout may be keying in on.

If you get to your favorite pool or run and see nothing rising, consider moving. For a long time, you could drive along the shoulder of the train tracks and no one said anything. Now the railroad has put up gates, making it harder to drive-and-hunt as you look for risers. It therefore pays to learn all the public access points, which will be abetted by the accompanying maps.

From late May through early July, the last 45 minutes of light can at times be breathtaking, with a dozen or more big fish materializing out of a seemingly dead river. Get yourself mentally and physically prepared, and stay until at least a little past dark. There is also occasionally some good morning activity, especially to those dependable tricos. In fact, some main-stem regulars think this trico action, which stretches for weeks, to be the next best thing to the Hendricksons.

Especially after July 1, local anglers with big nets (to land the fish) can be seen fishing after dark for rainbows better than 20 inches and browns a good deal better than that. Some use bait, but a great many use large wet flies. I am not a big night fisherman, but I've spent months worth of days

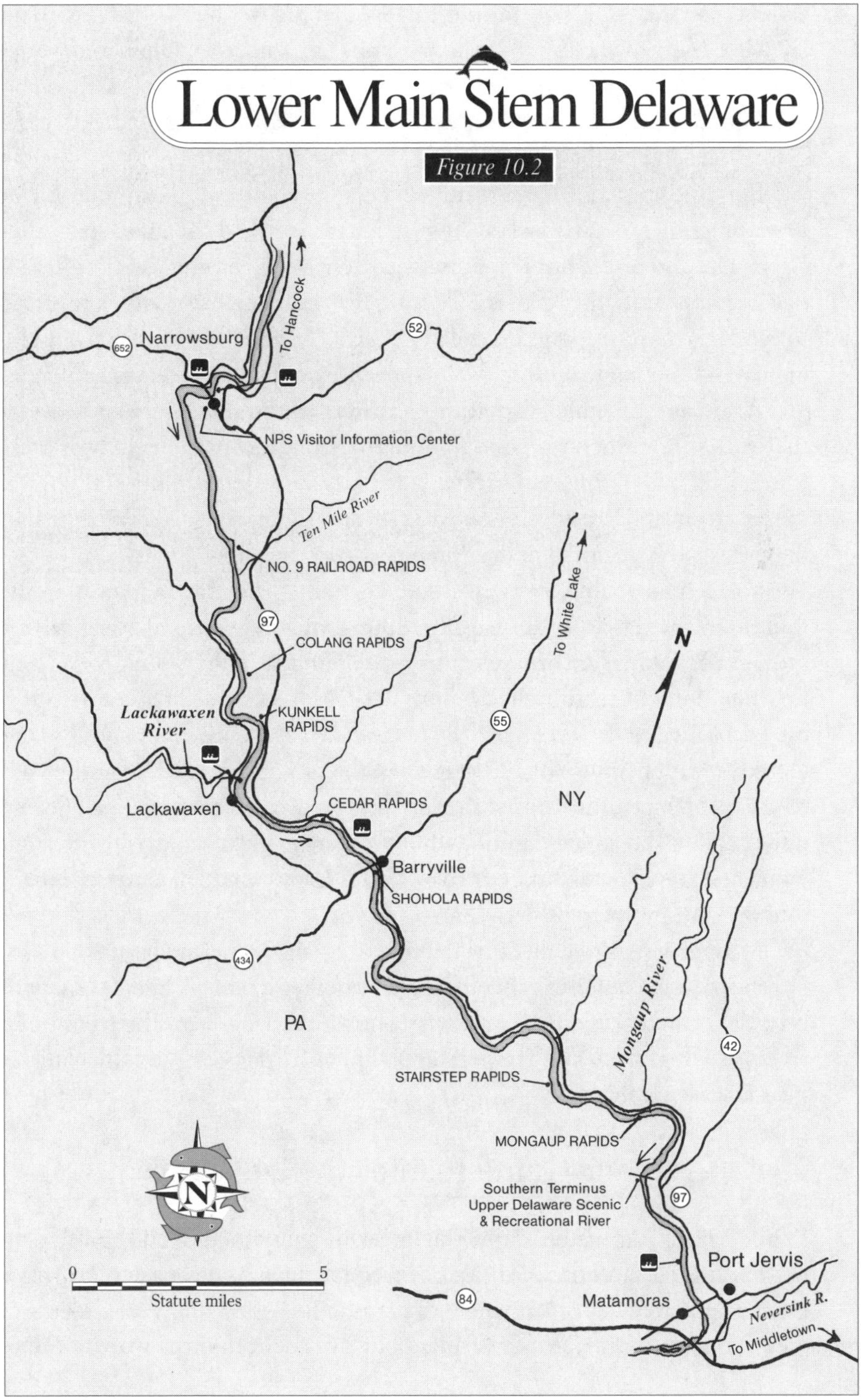

Lower Main Stem Delaware

Figure 10.2

To Hancock

652 Narrowsburg   52

NPS Visitor Information Center

Ten Mile River

NO. 9 RAILROAD RAPIDS

97   COLANG RAPIDS

To White Lake

Lackawaxen River   KUNKELL RAPIDS   55   **N**

Lackawaxen   CEDAR RAPIDS   NY

Barryville

SHOHOLA RAPIDS

434

PA   *Mongaup River*

42

STAIRSTEP RAPIDS

MONGAUP RAPIDS

Southern Terminus
Upper Delaware Scenic
& Recreational River   97

Port Jervis

0   5

Statute miles   84   Matamoras   *Neversink R.*

To Middletown

camping on the big Delaware and I know that big wet flies fished after dark are what many of the top fly-fishermen rely on. You can also use a topwater bug or small popper and fish it in the slower pools. Keep casting and twitching it enticingly on the surface. This is a tactic that I've used with good success on some of the bigger holes in the East Branch.

Both the weather and the water temperature cool very quickly after Labor Day, sometimes as early as late August. I haven't fished the main stem after Labor Day too often, but I've heard that things can get interesting. There is one late-season fly that comes off in August and September and is reported to evoke excellent feeding. It's called *Ephoron leukon,* a big, whitish fly. As I'll discuss in a moment, autumn fishing pressure on the main stem is very light.

Again as a possible adaptation to the realities of big water, or to water that varies in temperature due to unnatural and inconsistent tailwater releases, Delaware trout seem to feed at more extreme temperatures. If you get to the stream and the water is between 48 and 72 degrees, safely assume that there exists the potential of drumming up some business.

You can take rainbows here even on extremely hot days and even in the middle of the day in summer. One Fourth of July weekend I was with a group at Hankins, and we set out on a cooling, 5-mile tubing trip. I was floating along peacefully just below Basket Creek when I spied two fly-casters below me. It was one of the hottest days I've ever experienced in the Catskills, with readings of 103 degrees in the sun next to my tent and 96 degrees (true temperature) out of the sun. Yet the two die-hard gents we floated past each hooked a nice rainbow while we were in sight. One fish was about 14 inches, the other about 16 inches. I don't know what the water temperature was, but it had to be between 70 and 75.

Most experts agree that it is unethical to fish for thermally stressed fish, or fish that have sought shelter in a cold-water refugium. While I agree with this, I assume that if a fish is really stressed it probably won't be feeding. In any case, when the water temperature is above 72 degrees I usually hang up my rod and go tubing.

Other Game Fish of the Delaware

While I have just talked about the upper or trout zone of the main stem, what follows is not strictly a discussion of the lower part of the river below the primary trout zone. Rather, it is a general discussion, much of which will apply to both sections of the river.

TOBY McAFEE

A drift-boat trip with an experienced guide is the best way to introduce yourself to this large, imposing, and often difficult river.

Strictly by my own experience, smallmouths in the Delaware tend to be really runty, mostly under 11 inches. No one I personally know pursues them specifically. Still, one river fishing guide I spoke with claims that he and his clients take bronzebacks of more than 3 pounds with some consistency. He states that you really have to fish for them, that weather patterns are important, and that you really have to know where to look for the better ones. One lure he uses a lot is a popper. I should mention that this expert told me that the water below Callicoon is not necessarily better for bass. He says there are some profitable bass holes in the upper main stem, too.

Walleyes here average about 17 to 18 inches, but sports have netted fish up to about 12 pounds. Local sport shop owners generally agree that a 5- or 6-pounder is a very good fish. All the local experts I spoke with agreed that spring and fall are notably better for walleyes than is summer. Most thought late evening or night to be preferable for this glassy-eyed, nocturnal predator, though some seemed to think you can take them all day long if you know what you're doing. Some river guides do fish the walleyes. While there is almost certainly some natural reproduction of this species, the Pennsylvania Fish and Boat Commission does stock walleyes in parts of the main stem.

Shore lunch, during a July float trip on the main Delaware.

This to me is a questionable policy. The main stem is now essentially a wild-fish river. Today's more thoughtful angler wants to fish over wild trout and other species, and the opportunity exists to let the entire Delaware River below the dams be "all wild."

A good tactic is to drift the river in a canoe, vertically jigging through the deeper, stiller holes where the walleyes tend to congregate. Stay on the bottom—that's where the fish are almost all the time. (*Note:* I have heard that in some of the extremely deep, large pools at Narrowsburg and below, walleyes actually suspend, and that here trolling is popular. The sport shop owner who told me this recommended using a depth finder.) A traditional walleye bait in the Delaware is a baby lamprey, which I've heard can be dug up in certain river sandbars. Check on the current legality of this.

A jig tipped with a whole nightcrawler can be dynamic, too. Other lures and baits include grub tails, slender jigging spoons with or without bait, and a June Bug spinner–worm combo. One local expert says live minnows work as well as anything, and he especially likes to fish them in the deep holes in autumn from a canoe. Here we're talking about October and November when, I've heard, the walleyes become very active. Walleye fans I've spoken with also tout minnow-type lures like the Rapala. A floating model, which will dive quite deep anyway, will reduce snags, while a "walking" sinker ahead of the lure will bring it down to the fish's level. Whatever type of weight you use, a three-way swivel can figure in such bottom rigs. But the three-ways tend to tangle so much that I think a better rig is a simple slip-sinker rig with a hook or lure at the end, a barrel swivel 2 feet above the bait, and the slip or egg sinker just above this.

I do believe this, though: You need a boat for walleyes. No matter how you fish from shore, if you're near the bottom where you should be you're going to get snagged constantly. Lures are too expensive to lose on every other cast, and the nuisance of retying bait rigs every five minutes just may not be worth it.

American shad *(Alosa sapidisima)* make a spawning run into the Delaware in spring, and are highly prized as a sport fish. They are extremely good eating when boned, but I can't say for sure whether there is some stage during the spawning season at which their flesh is less palatable. I have eaten the roe of females that I caught in the Delaware, and it was just as good as roe I've purchased in fish markets in early spring.

Sportsmen pursue them from well down in New Jersey all the way up through the main stem and even into the East Branch. I've taken them as far upriver as McCarter's Run on the East Branch, and the pool just above this—the Shad Pool—got its name for obvious reasons. They have, in fact, been observed right on up to the Pepacton dam at Downsville. Until the Delaware was fully developed and promoted as a trout fishery, shad was the most popular sport fish on the big Delaware. The peak of the run is early May below Callicoon, and mid- to late May above Callicoon and in the East Branch. Some fish are taken well into June. In the most recent season, officials say that shad were abundant in the lower main stem, but they apparently did not ascend the river as far as usual. Perhaps slight variations in water temperature or flow rate have some effect on shad behavior in any given year.

Keep your shad spinning tackle light—4- to 6-pound test. One-fourth-ounce leadhead jigs in white/yellow or yellow/red are the standard weapons, but carry some smaller, $1/8$-ounce jigs, too. Fly-fishermen use special fluorescent or otherwise gaudy wet flies and streamers and cast, if possible, to a visible grouping of fish. You have to taunt the nonfeeding shad. Keep dancing or just hovering that fly in front of his face.

One evening in early July I was casting a Mepps spinner in the riffle just below Kellam's Bridge. In midstream, something walloped the lure and ripped viciously downstream. Through the 10-minute fight, I kept thinking breathlessly that I'd finally hooked up with a 5-pound Delaware River rainbow. I even saw what I thought was crimson when the fish turned in the current, but it was not to be. It was a prime buck shad, proving at least three things: Shad will take spinning lures, they can be caught in summer, and suckers aren't the only fish that make suckers out of fishermen.

The American eel is common in the Delaware, and believe it or not, there are a few anglers who go after these slimy critters. There are even a few commercial eel fishermen left here, a remnant of a once-thriving river industry. I finally met in person a Delaware River eel fisherman! He has a cabin near Basket Creek, and claims that eels taste better than any trout that ever lived. I lend full support to the thought, and rank smoked eel near the very top of my favorite gourmet exotica. Smoked Delaware River eels are available in some river communities. I've found them in Barryville and Port Jervis, and now there is a smokehouse on the East Branch just above Hancock.

I've tubed the river for miles, often with my face right down to the water. You might be interested to know that to date I have seen bass, sunfish, sea lampreys, shad, eels, rock bass, yellow perch, and various minnows. No walleyes, though. I think they hide deep and under the rocks in the daytime, although a friend of mine has seen them while snorkeling here. And no trout,

The author plays a nice rainbow in thin riffle water at Hankins.
Stoneflies are among the insects that take to this fast water;
fish appropriate imitations on a short line.

either. I can't say why. Maybe they're just warier and flee at my approach.

The big Delaware from Callicoon down to Port Jervis is primarily a warm-water river. There is surely a fair amount of effort expended on shad in springtime, but after that the river is very lightly fished. Remember, this is a stretch of some 45 miles of essentially unspoiled river. That's a lot of opportunity for anyone who wants to angle for scrappy smallmouths or tasty walleyes with extremely little competition from other fishermen. True, many canoeists take a rod along with them, but most of them aren't serious fishermen. Serious anglers on the lower main stem after the shad run are extremely scarce.

For reasons no one is sure about, striped bass have been penetrating the upper Delaware River for about a decade or more, and anglers have taken fish of at least 38 inches. Many people are guessing that cleaner water around the Philadelphia–Trenton area has simply eliminated the "pollution block" that had stopped the stripers previously. In any case, like the shad, this premier saltwater sport fish spends part of its life in brackish or freshwater rivers or estuaries, so a run up into the Delaware cannot be seen as an anomaly. One report I had is that they are most common in the deeper pools of the Delaware, and are almost always taken by anglers trying for other species.

Some have speculated that the striped bass could damage the wild-rainbow fishery, but there is not yet evidence of this happening.

Already there are a couple of entertaining stories circulating about fly-fishermen having hooked a nice trout only to have it disappear in a great, biblical swirl. It's a delicious irony: purist fly-fisher turned into bait-fisher after all.

A few years ago the Pennsylvania Fish and Boat Commission and the National Park Service jointly conducted angler use and fish harvest surveys on the main stem Delaware between Hankins Creek and Sparrowbush. From these surveys came some interesting statistics on both the fish and the fishing in the lower river. They showed, for one thing, just how dominant the shad fishery is. From mid-April through June, 96 percent of the anglers interviewed were fishing for shad, and 33 percent had caught at least one fish. The harvested fish averaged 6 pounds apiece.

Walleyes were second in importance during this spring period. In fact, 98 percent of the total walleyes harvested from April 10 through October 17 were taken during this spring period. That is certainly strong support of the belief that summertime walleye fishing is not easy. The walleyes in the survey, by the way, averaged 2 to 3 pounds.

In summer and autumn, interest turned overwhelmingly to smallmouth bass (remember: The survey covered the Delaware below the principal trout zone). Here there are some very telling statistics. Of the 28,155 bass caught, only 8,494 were kept. The reason undoubtedly was the size of the fish—they averaged only about ¾ pound apiece. As with all main-stem fish, angler pressure on smallies was very light in autumn, even though bass season here is year-round. Interestingly, a number of fishermen interviewed were fishing specifically for the good-tasting American eel. One person was trying specifically for carp.

It should be apparent from all this that, after shad season, smallmouth bass are the most catchable game fish on the lower main stem.

A little background on the main Delaware would be in order. In 1978 Congress designated 73.4 miles of the upper Delaware River as one of our National Wild and Scenic Rivers. It begins just below Hancock and ends downstream near Mill Rift, Pennsylvania. The Wild and Scenic Rivers Act states that the river must be protected in its free-flowing condition and that water quality and natural resources must be preserved for the benefit and enjoyment of present and future generations. The National Park Service now administers this part of the Delaware, which is correctly called the Upper

Delaware Scenic and Recreational River. The river is now much better protected—though by no means completely so—from development and other human degradation.

Access to the main stem is a subject that needs discussion. The Upper Delaware is quite unusual among National Park Service units (it's not technically a park) in that the NPS does not own any significant amount of land along the river—only about 30 acres. This includes a few acres at its headquarters in Narrowsburg, a small parcel at Roebling Bridge, and the Zane Grey House and Museum in Lackawaxen, Pennsylvania. Most of the rest of the river corridor is privately owned, though there are a couple of state forest or game management lands owned by New York or Pennsylvania that touch or nearly touch the river and that, being public lands, thereby afford river access. At present, a decreasing amount of riverbank property remains unposted. In New York State you may legally fish along a waterway that is not posted, even though it is always a desirable courtesy to ask permission of the owner. Yet despite short stretches of unposted land and the possibility of using local side roads to gain access, much of the upper main stem and a lot of the lower main stem cannot legally be approached on foot.

That leads to the NPS and other agencies that are establishing public access points along the main stem. For the most part, an access site allows you to launch or take out your canoe (or drift boat, float tube, raft) and fish at that point and for a very short way up- or downstream, depending on the boundaries of the access site. Of course, everyone else fishes at these access points too. I've boldfaced the names of the sites, which are sometimes the same as the village they are in or near. New sites, I should mention, are still being developed.

The facilities at these sites vary. For example, some have picnic tables and rest rooms, and others don't. An important one is at **Skinners Falls** below Cochecton on the New York side. Owned by the DEC but administered by the NPS, it has a "kiosk" or little information center where literature is posted and where—depending on the season and day of the week—NPS personnel may be in attendance to offer advice and help. Another kiosk is at the **Ten Mile River** site, located where the Ten Mile River meets the Delaware River below Narrowsburg.

At Narrowsburg and at a couple of other places, the river is big enough that a motorboat can be feasibly launched and used. I discourage the practice, since any part of the Delaware discussed in this chapter can be easily covered with a canoe or rowboat.

On the Pennsylvania side, the Pennsylvania Fish and Boat Commission has established several river access points: **Shehawken**—just below Hancock—a canoe and fishing access site; **Buckingham**—above Equinunk—rest rooms and boat launch; **Callicoon**—at Callicoon—rest rooms and boat launch; **Damascus**—at Damascus—rest rooms and boat launch; **Narrowsburg**—across the river from Narrowsburg—rest rooms and boat launch; and **Lackawaxen**—just upriver from Lackawaxen—rest rooms, boat launch, and NPS-staffed kiosk.

While none of these parcels on either side of the river is large, each will permit some shore fishing, and boats can always be launched for free. Note that both New York and Pennsylvania sites are open to all citizens, though you must have either a New York or a Pennsylvania fishing license to fish any part of the main stem, from a boat or from shore. All motorized or commercial boats using Pennsylvania accesses must be registered through the Pennsylvania Fish and Boat Commission.

The National Park Service is an excellent starting point for further information on the main stem. Its mailing address is R.R. 2, Box 2428, Beach Lake, PA 18405, and its headquarters is on River Road about 1.5 miles north of the Narrowsburg bridge on the Pennsylvania side of the river. The headquarters is open to the public Monday through Friday from 8:30 A.M. to 5 P.M., and there is some literature on display, but a broader selection of materials, including books, may be found at the NPS Information Center on Main Street in Narrowsburg. National Park Service suboffices are located in Milanville, Pennsylvania, and about 2 miles south of Barryville, New York, on Route 97. Here, too, you can pick up literature and have a question or two answered. Finally, the NPS has a well-developed web site wherein you will find much useful information and key links. It is provided on page 211.

The NPS already offers some good free literature, partially listed below. New pieces are always being developed, so check on what, pertinent to the angler, might be available that's not listed here.

One final thought: You will not find well-stocked, active sport and tackle shops in all the Delaware River communities. I am aware of shops in Port Jervis, Lackawaxen, Narrowsburg, Callicoon, and Hankins, and I'm sure there are others. Some of these shops may well be closed in the off-season, or even on weekdays at the fringes of the season. Many general stores and hardware stores in the area also sell some tackle.

Here are a few NPS publications that would be useful to fishermen (all free).

1. "Upper Delaware Official Map and Guide"

An excellent map that shows the river plus all roads, towns, boat launch/access sites, rest rooms, campgrounds, picnic areas, and more. This was used as the base map for the maps presented in this chapter, and its size allows for more detail than we were able to show.

2. *Map and Guide for Touring the Upper Delaware*

An excellent combination map–brochure published by the Upper Delaware Council and distributed by the council and NPS. Unlike the above map, it lists area restaurants, accommodations, boat liveries, and so on.

3. *Fishing the Upper Delaware*

A single-page brochure, updated yearly, that contains information about licenses, seasons, access. It includes black-and-white drawings of all the popular sport fish of the Delaware's main stem.

A Floater's Odyssey

If you have a canoe, a tent, and some time to spare, you can spend a magnificent and inexpensive five days on the Delaware. A nice time to do this—when good water flows, good fishing, and pleasant camping conditions are most likely to fall together—is the first 10 days of June. See the discussion in chapter 9 about water-release policies on the Delaware system. You can also call the campgrounds at which you'll be staying to get a feel for the condition of the rivers.

All the campgrounds named here are privately owned. All take day-to-day tenters at present, but a regional trend in camping is toward "all seasonals." Of course you'll find this out when you call to make your advance reservations. This is the peak of the fly-fishing season, so go on weekdays if at all possible. It will make a huge difference.

Because you're using a canoe you do not need any actual boat launches, but you will need two people in reasonably good shape to jockey the canoe up and down the riverbank in a few instances. I've selected spots where the efforts called for are reasonable. The maps presented in chapter 9 and in this chapter include little letters that are keyed to this text.

You'll need two cars to pull this off. Early on day 1, or the night before, check in at the Delaware River Club (see chapter 9) and set up your tent if you wish. Take one car down to the Buckingham access on the Pennsylvania side of the main stem (A on figure 10.1), and take the other car with the canoe up to the Balls Eddy access on the Pennsylvania side of the West

Branch (B on figure 9.2). You're going to spend a leisurely but full day floating and fishing the fish-filled lower end of the West Branch and the best part of the main stem. End at Buckingham, put the canoe on the car, then head into Hancock for the provisions you'll need for the next few days (there's a full-sized supermarket here). You will be spending the night at the Delaware River Club's camping area.

Get up early on day 2, because you have a long day ahead of you. Leave your tent set up at the campground and take both cars. Leave one car at the large parking area on the East Branch of the Delaware exactly where Cadosia Creek enters (C on figure 9.1) This is just outside the village of Hancock. Take the canoe, all your fishing gear, and your lunch in the other car. Drive east on the Quickway until you get to the exit for East Branch. This is the point at which Route 30, Route 17, and old Route 17 all meet. Right here, at the junction of the Beaver Kill and the East Branch, there is adequate parking on the shoulder of old Route 17 (D on figure 9.1). You're going to spend the day floating and fishing almost the entire lower section of the East Branch.

After launching you almost immediately come to a spot known as The Jaws, which relatively few people fish. The backwashes normally yield only unimpressive smallmouths, but I've taken some eye-popping rainbows in these admittedly thin riffles. Fish the famous pools down from here, including the Beaverdell Pool (there is a tavern by it), the Shad Pool (behind the rest area), and McCarter's Run, pulling the canoe over frequently and whenever you spot rising fish. It's generally easier to wade than to fish from a canoe. If you like shad and it's the season, fish the rest area pool well. If it's green drake time, this long, slow pool is the place to be.

Continue on down to Fish's Eddy. Just below the steel trestle there is a spectacular pool that is also a good place to fish for shad. From this point down you are far more likely to encounter rainbows than browns. If you started early enough in the morning, you will have time to fish some of the long pools or "eddies" for which the lower East Branch is famous. One section of this river that is quite lightly fished is the big bend at Pea's Eddy. In summer this lower end of the East Branch gets very warm, and the trout may migrate out of it. For this reason, I recommend you do the float earlier in the season.

By and by you will come to Cadosia Creek. While it is a little rocky here, taking out the canoe should not be a problem. If time permits, fish near the mouth of Cadosia Creek, in the nice long run below this, and in the short pocket-sized pools just above Cadosia Creek. Head back up to East Branch to get the other car, and then make your way back to camp.

The next morning, day 3 of your odyssey, break camp; you will then have some jockeying to do. Both drivers head down to Callicoon on Route 97 on the New York side. The car without the canoe is left at the Upper Delaware River Campground (E on figure 10.1) in Callicoon. Tell the campground staffers your plans, then take the canoe and the fishing and camping gear in the other car back up to the Delaware River Club. By prior arrangment, ask someone with the club to follow you to the Buckingham access then take your second car back to the Delaware River Club, where it will be left. If you explain your itinerary they should be cooperative, and the fee they charge you will be worth it. If this option does not pan out, you'll have to use your ingenuity.

Sometimes we've tried to launch at Buckingham and had our plans thrown off by nice trout rising right at the launch site! But even if you're asail by midmorning, you will have time to reach your evening's destination, the Soaring Eagle Campground (F on figure 10.1) at Kellam's Bridge on the Pennsylvania side of the main stem.

Many guides concentrate on that part of the main stem between Hancock and Buckingham, but there are plenty of trout below this. Today you're going to see more of this glorious big water.

There are innumerable nice spots to fish along this reach of river. One of the deepest pools on the upper main stem is right at Equinunk (G on figure 10.1), where a guide I know once took a 4-pound smallmouth—the biggest he's ever caught in the river. There are also walleyes in this hole. Although many canoeists don't think of it, it's nice to have an anchor on board for those places you can't wade, or for when you just don't feel like getting out of the canoe.

Continue downstream and you'll encounter much nice water between Lordville and Long Eddy. I especially like the water below Lordville where the main stem makes a sharp bend to the north (H on figure 10.1). It's quite wild looking here, and there are both nice riffles and nice pools.

Continue on down and spend a little time fishing the series of riffles below Basket Creek, marked clearly by the high Route 97 bridge. There is a nice run on the east bank just below Basket Creek (letter I on figure 10.1), and the riffles just below this always offer the promise of a few hard-fighting rainbows. After a bit of a deadwater, the river's slope again increases and you have more productive riffle water to fish, just above and at the Soaring Eagle Campground. After checking in and setting up your tent, fish the evening hours on those productive riffles out front, or in the huge pool just below Kellam's Bridge.

The next morning, have a big camp breakfast and sleep late if you've found a few new muscles. Then get ready on this, day 4, to see more nice trout water on the big Delaware. First, devote a good hour to the Kellam's Bridge Pool, where trout are often seen rising. This pool is so large that it's best fished from the canoe. When you've had enough here, paddle quickly through the deadwater just below Kellam's, watching for cardinal flowers on the bank if it's early summer. You're now into some nice rainbow riffles. Fish these (J on figure 10.1) by beaching your canoe at convenient points. Move slowly or you'll spook the blue heron. You probably won't bother the merganser clans too much, though. After this, move on down through another long deadwater to the renowned "Campground Pool" at the Red Barn Campground in Hankins (which now, regrettably, accepts only seasonals). Because of all the camper activity, midday is not the best time to fish this pool, but a hatch can happen at any time here, and when it does, fish will rise even if there is commotion in the water. The lower end of the pool, just as you're passing the campground, is more lightly fished and less disturbed by swimmers, tubers, snorkelers, and other summer revelers.

If it's now only early afternoon, you can take your time and savor the broadly flowing water between Hankins and Callicoon. This is big, majestic trout water on the order of a Western river, and the scenic views are captivating. While you may be nearing the lower end of the best trout water, some exciting trout moments are still to be had on this beat of river.

Check in at the Upper Delaware River Campground and take a well-deserved nap in your tent. If you don't feel like cooking, head up Route 97 a few miles to Club 97, a well-established local restaurant with a good reputation and some delicious homemade pies. Then retrieve the other car at the Delaware River Club.

The next morning, day 5, sleep in, then have a big breakfast to the melody of the river flowing by. You can end your trip now, but if you wish to extend it to the full five days, here's a plan.

First, drive into Callicoon (you can practically walk it) to Peck's market and buy whatever provisions you might need. Then head up to Basket Creek to the Andersen farm and get a quart of local maple syrup for your next pancake breakfast. The provisions thus in, spend the rest of the day fishing the big river on foot—or take in some of the local attractions, such as the Zane Grey House or Roebling Bridge. For a great selection of brochures and regional books, stop at the National Park Service Visitor Center in Narrows-burg.

If you fancy smaller water, try Callicoon Creek, which joins the main stem practically at your campground. See chapter 7.

The above is, of course, a trout fisherman's float. To extend your odyssey from five to six or seven days you can continue on down from Callicoon, leaving a car ahead of you and camping along the way. Here you'll find small-mouth bass and walleye, and even a few trout, especially in spring. Just re-member that below Callicoon there are some Class II and mild Class III rapids that should be scouted, or avoided by absolute novice canoeists.

Resources

1. New York State Department of Environmental Conservation (DEC)
Manages all the waters of the state of New York, and offers many well-written publications.

Region 3—Westchester, Putnam, Rockland, Dutchess, Orange, Ulster, and Sullivan Counties
21 South Putt Corners Road
New Paltz, NY 12561

Region 4—Delaware, Greene, Otsego, Schoharie, Montgomery, Albany, Rensselaer, and Columbia Counties
Route 10, H.C.R. 1
Stamford, NY 12167

Web site for all DEC regions: www.dec.state.ny.us

2. National Park Service, Upper Delaware River Unit
Administers the Upper Delaware Scenic and Recreational River

R.R. 2, Box 2428
Beach Lake, PA 18405
www.nps.gov/upde

3. U.S. Geological Survey
Provides stream flow rates
http://water.usgs.gov/ny/nwis/rt
Note: rt here stands for real time. This site has been subject to change, but if you go to the main site up to and including gov, you should be able to find real-time flow rates for the Beaver Kill, the Delaware, and possibly other important Catskill rivers.

Index

Books from The Countryman Press
and Backcountry Guides

We offer many more books on hiking, bicycling, canoeing and kayaking, travel, nature, and country living. Our books are available at bookstores and outdoor stores everywhere. For more information or a free catalog, please call 1-800-245-4151, or write to us at The Countryman Press, P.O. Box 748, Woodstock, Vermont 05091. You can find us on the Internet at www.countrymanpress.com